INSIGHT COMPACT GUIDES

FLORENCE

Compact Guide: Florence is the ultimate quick-reference guide to this city of the Renaissance. It tells you all you need to know about Florence's magnificent attractions, from the Uffizi Gallery to the Ponte Vecchio, from Michelangelo's David to Brunelleschi's Duomo.

This is just one title in *Apa Publications'* new series of pocket-sized, easy-to-use guidebooks intended for the independent-minded traveller. Based on an award-winning formula pioneered in Germany, *Compact Guides* pride themselves on being up-to-date and authoritative. They are in essence mini travel encyclopedias, designed to be comprehensive yet portable, both readable and reliable.

Star Attractions

An instant reference to some of Florence's most popular tourist attractions to help you on your way.

Baptistry doors p16

Duomo p18

Michelangelo's Pietà p25

Piazza della Signoria p26

Palazzo Vecchio p27

David p61

Galleria degli Uffizi p32

Ponte Vecchio p43

Brancacci Chapel p45

Santa Croce p71

Florence

Introduction

Places

Culture

Leisure

Practical Information

Florence – Cradle of the Renaissance

Opposite: corridor linking the Uffizi to Ponte Vecchio

During the hot summer months, it is a struggle to walk from the Duomo to Piazza della Signoria. A mauve heat haze hangs in the air and damp crowds sway blindly past the golden buildings.

In the sacred tourist triangle of Italian cities, Florence beats Venice and Rome in popularity: over 8 million people visit the city every year. Every second person appears to be a tourist searching in vain for one of the city's four nude Davids. (Michelangelo's sculpture is in the Accademia but copies stand outside the Palazzo Vecchio and on Piazzale Michelangelo; Donatello's more subdued David is in the Bargello).

Florence is arguably the most beautiful city in Italy; and certainly the most harmonious. The city was largely rebuilt during the Renaissance and maintains its elegantly rational urban design. In its heyday, in the 14th and 15th centuries, Florence was considered the most innovative artistic centre in Europe. Today, the Uffizi would be the world's greatest gallery of Renaissance art – if the city of Florence itself did not lay claim to the accolade.

David at the Palazzo Vecchio

5

Reflected glory

The city on the Arno

The capital of Tuscany is set in the Arno river valley 50m (164ft) above sea-level. Florence has the valley basin and protective chain of hills to thank for its mild climate. Only in July and August, when the valley is stifling and the nights prone to thunderstorms, do conditions become uncomfortable. Then it is best to follow the Florentines, if only for the afternoon, in leaving the city heat haze for Fiesole or any spot in the cool encircling hills.

The city's changing face

Like Rome, Florence was founded at the narrowest point of a river. It is curious to think that it all began with an administrative decision in Rome: a colony of Roman army veterans founded Florentia (Florence) on the banks of the Arno in 59BC, overlooked by the wealthy colony of Fiesole, a site still rich in Roman remains.

Florence survived the Roman Empire but really flourished in the Middle Ages. The city's prosperity was founded on the medieval cloth trade, with imported wool processed and exported from the city. Florentine merchants controlled the market by securing trade routes, setting fixed rates of mercantile interest and getting exemption from foreign levies.

The pace of Florence's shift from feudalism to mercantilism outstripped most cities. Such success was the product of a clear civic identity, enterprise, an enlightened view of commerce and an intuitive grasp of banking. In

Florentine bankers

Palazzo Vecchio

1115 Florence was granted the status of a *comune*, an independent city, governed by a council drawn from the mercantile class. The merchant families settled legal disputes and, despite sharp clashes and factionalism, the common good prevailed.

The council, which eventually sat in the Palazzo Vecchio, became known as the Signoria. Today Piazza della Signoria is still Florence's grandest square and Palazzo Vecchio, the magnificent Gothic town hall, remains the hub of Florentine life, the place for state banquets, traffic debates, or simply the place for ordinary citizens to renew their residence permits.

Through its wealth, architectural and artistic creations, Florence had already laid the foundation for the Renaissance by the early 1300s. By 1252 there were three new bridges over the Arno, and during the decades that followed, the buildings that dominate the cityscape today were constructed. After building the Bargello, the first seat of government and the residence of the chief of police, the city commissioned the Palazzo Vecchio, a more sumptuous town hall, and the Duomo (1296), an Italian cathedral second only to St Peter's in size and splendour.

Urban expansion went hand in hand with the city's territorial gains, as Florence became the major political power of the region. Expansion without subjugation was the Florentine watchword. By the end of the 14th century, the cities of Pistoia, Prato, San Gimignano, Volterra and Arezzo were brought into the Florentine orbit. The capture of Pisa in 1406 brought a coveted sea port, a gain followed by Cortona (1411) and Livorno (1421). Siena, the illustrious city state, stood out against Florentine domination until 1555. Lucca was the sole Tuscan city to escape absorption by Florence.

City of the arts

Florence thrived on artistic patronage, from the city rulers downwards. Large-scale projects were paid for by the powerful banking and wool merchant guilds, both to glorify the city and themselves. Acting on the same principle, the ruling Medici dynasty later commissioned the greatest Renaissance artists and sculptors, from Donatello and Michelozzo to Botticelli and Michelangelo. On a smaller scale, wealthy Florentine families took great pride in the numbers of richly decorated chapels they added to the city's churches.

Clues to the source of this patronage can be found everywhere in Florence. For example, on the Doors of Paradise on the Baptistry, in the centre panel on the right, a sack can be seen – the symbol of mercantile wealth. The original panels are now in the Museo dell'Opera del Duomo. Profits were made then just as they are now, the difference being that the medieval mind had a guilty conscience about money-making. Charitable religious foundations helped to assuage such doubts, however, and the regular purchase of security beyond the grave allowed the arts to flourish. Thus it was that the city of the arts was founded on the guilty conscience of the merchant class.

Masaccio's Adam and Eve

The competitiveness of the guilds and city factions was a spur to artistic endeavour. Also at stake was the prestige of the city. The collective urban identity, known as *campanilismo* (literally the attachment to one's own bell-tower), fostered a unique desire to glorify Florence, to show that it was the greatest of city states. This fervour, combined with a heady intellectual climate, the re-evaluation of classical ideas, the presence of wealthy patrons and a supremely gifted pool of artists – all these strands melded in the miracle of the Florentine Renaissance.

City of science

The Renaissance was not only distinguished by a strong interest in the arts; the natural sciences exercised an equally powerful fascination. Renaissance architects Filippo Brunelleschi and Leon Battista Alberti wrote theoretical works based on their studies of the classical world. Florence was sometimes referred to as 'Athens on the Arno'. During its long reign (from 1530 onwards), the Medici dynasty maintained an interest in the natural sciences alongside its penchant for art collecting. Leonardo da Vinci was commissioned to decorate their court. In 1610, Galileo Galilei discovered the moons of Jupiter with his astronomical telescope and named them the *pianeti medici* after his benefactors. In 1545 Cosimo I, a Medici ruler, had one of the world's first botanical gardens designed for medicinal purposes.

The Florentine legacy

As well as the discoveries made by Renaissance artists and scientists, there were major literary milestones. The Florentines were at the forefront of literary endeavour and championed the use of the vernacular, with Italian literature of the period equated with Florentine literature. Dante and Boccaccio chose to write in the Florentine dialect rather than in Latin, a dialect that became recognised as standard Italian.

In the field of politics, Machiavelli's name is as relevant as ever, with *The Prince*, his manual of statecraft, a classic of the genre. In terms of banking, Florence was a world leader and devised such procedures as double-entry book-keeping. The Medici and Bardi monopolised the money markets of the day while the first florin, named after the city, was minted in 1252 and quickly became an international currency.

Every building a work of art

Outdoor café

City of fashion

Certainly, the Florentine legacy embraces artistic innovation, a revival of humanistic values, bold new scientific thinking and vivid literature. Yet the legacy is more than the sum of its parts: at its fullest, it can only be termed 'the Florentine miracle', a unique combination of circumstances that caused a flowering of the human spirit.

Florence today

After sleeping its way through post-Renaissance social change, Florence was discovered by enthusiastic Grand Tourists in the 18th century, and the wave of arrivals has not abated. Over-exposure to enraptured visitors has confirmed blasé Florentines in their world view, one that is essentially aloof, superior and provincial. Today's population of 300,000 is happy to profit from tourism but is often reluctant to pay the price. '*Porta aperta a chi porta*' runs the local saying: 'the door is open to those bringing gifts'; and restaurateurs are eager to open their doors to tourists, the golden geese.

The pull of its artistic heritage risks turning Florence into 'the city with some of the finest car-parks in the world'. Fortunately, after years of deliberation, the council recently introduced a ban on city centre traffic: a partial success, despite the presence of some private cars and the profusion of (unbanned) *motorini* (motor bikes).

Certain far-reaching town-planning decisions are inevitable, however, if Florence is not to become an open-air museum. Enough residential and commercial space must be made available to keep the city's medium-sized firms and their employees from leaving. The long-term strategy is for the historic centre to remain the cultural heart, with the commercial centre moved to the northwest, towards the new city airport of Peretola. The satellite towns of Firenze Nova and Novoli are under construction but few administrative offices have moved yet.

Florence never became a modern industrial powerhouse. Instead, its self-confident mercantile tradition never died out, and the city has enthusiastically embraced the service sector. Apart from the tentacles of the tourist industry, Florence hosts trade fairs and congresses yet remains a noted craft centre. The Oltrarno district, on the quieter side of the Arno, is an enticing place for pottering in search of hand-tooled marbled paper, leather goods, striking jewellery or antiques. On the chic side of the Arno, the discreet elegance of the boutiques on Via Tornabuoni is a sign of the highly-developed Florentine aesthetic sense. Florentine fashion still commands attention, as the names Gucci, Pucci and Ferragamo imply. World history may be made in Rome; fashion and design may be centred on Milan; but Florence will forever be the capital of classic good taste.

History: the Key Players

Early settlers

Archaeological finds have proved that the ford across the river not far from today's Ponte Vecchio was in use as far back as prehistoric times. The Etruscans began laying out the massive stone walls at Fiesole (now a suburb of Florence) in the late 7th century BC, long before the Latins ever settled on the Arno's banks. Throughout Tuscany, Etruscan villages, harbours, tombs and statuary testify to a remarkable and often overlooked civilisation, to which the vitality of 15th-century Florentine art owes a great deal. Some fine examples of Etruscan art are contained in Florence's Archaaeological Museum, including the celebrated bronzes, the *Arringatore* and the *Chimera*.

The actual date for the founding of Florence is generally agreed to be 59BC. The *Lex Iulia* gave land to Caesar's distinguished veterans, and *Florentia* (literally: the flourishing town) was designed in the fashion of a Roman *castrum*, ie a walled-in rectangle laid out like a chess-board and intersected by a grid of streets. *Florentia* was an important junction for the Roman network of main roads, a fact which ensured the steady growth of the city during the centuries that followed.

The merchant class

As early as the 11th century, Florentine merchants began importing wool from Northern Europe and rare dye-stuffs from the Mediterranean and the east. The wool trade swiftly beacme the city's biggest source of income, an industry that employed approximately one-third of her inhabitants by 1250.

Communal self-confidence gave rise to calls for independence, and after the death of Countess Matilda of Tuscany in 1115 Florence effectively became a City State, ruled by a council drawn from the merchant class. In 1125, the city flexed its mussles by capturing and destroying Fiesole. Soaring profits fuelled that other Florentine mainstay, banking. Financiers exploited the established trade routes and in 1252 a tiny gold coin was minted in the city that beacme the recognised unit of international currency, the florin.

Capitalism and expansion served to fuel the long-standing battle for territory and temporal power between the Guelfs, who supported the pope, and the Ghibellines who supported the Holy Roman Emperor. In Florence, the parties fought in the streets, attacking their enemies and retreating to the fortified palaces they had built.

By the end of the 13th century, the main issue was not political any longer: all that mattered was who controlled Florence. The *parte guelfa* absorbed the wealthy nobility, and the *arti* (guilds) represented the people and created the government (*signoria*). It was not long, however, before the rich patricians in the *parte guelfa* had started to squabble amongst themselves, and they split into *neri* and *bianchi* (Black Guelfs and White Guelfs) – the former close allies of the pope, the latter more conservative. Both attempted to influence the formation of the government. In 1302 the great poet Dante Alighieri, a White Guelf, was banned from the city for life along with 600 of his colleagues by a *signoria* sympathetic to the Black Guelf cause.

By the beginning of the 1400s, the guilds had begun to find new ways of expressing the rivalry that had previously caused so much bloodshed. Patronage of the arts became a new source of prestige. The wool-importers' guild set the precedent by its lavish expenditure on the Baptistry and its competition to choose the best artist to design the great bronze doors. Florence duly became the fountainhead of the Renaissance.

The Medici

The rise to power of the Medici family had been a quiet one: the banking family did not compete for high office, but instead increased its wealth immeasurably in its role as trustee of the Church's funds in Rome – in 1397 the family moved its headquarters from Rome to Florence.

The Medicis' policy in Florence was to pull strings quietly in the background, and it was only in 1421 that Giovanni di Bicci de' Medici assumed the highest office in the Republic. The Medici were respected by the people and feared by the city's other families, above all by the Albizi. After Bicci's death in 1429 the power struggle broke out into the open. In 1432 the Albizi managed to have the Medici expelled, but the latter promptly returned in 1434 and exiled the Albizi instead.

Bicci's heir Cosimo the Elder pulled strings, using money and diplomacy, and preferring to work privately in the background. He promoted humanism and donated money to churches and monasteries, keeping a cell for himself in San Marco. He founded the Medici dynasty that ruled Florence and Tuscany as a Grand Duchy until 1737 (and without a break from 1530), and included a long line of illustrious personalities.

Historical Highlights

59BC The colony of Florentia is founded. Rome gives land to Caesar's veterans. The *ager florentinus* extends as far as the Prato.

c AD250 St Miniato is martyred during the persecution of Christians under the Emperor Decius.

284–305 Florentia becomes the capital of Tuscany/Umbria under the Emperor Diocletian.

5th century The city is repeatedly sacked by Goths and Byzantines.

541 Florence captured by Byzantine troops.

570 Lombards occupy Tuscany, ruling Florence from Lucca. There ensue two centuries of peace, during which the Baptistry is built.

774 Charlemagne, the Frankish king, defeats the Lombards and appoints a margrave to rule Tuscany, still based in Lucca.

854 The county of Fiesole merges with that of Florence, and the city gains land.

c 1000 Margrave Ugo moves his court to Florence, which soon becomes a prosperous trading town.

1059 Baptistry consecrated by Pope Nicholas II; work begins on San Miniato al Monte.

1077 Pope Gregory VII, who comes from Tuscany, humiliates Emperor Henry IV at the castle of Canossa, home of Countess Matilda of Tuscany.

1115 After Matilda of Canossa's death the Comune di Firenze is formed; consuls and a 100-member council run the city. Important questions are brought before the *parlamento*.

1125 Fiesole is attacked and annexed by Florence.

1172 The new city wall encloses an area three times the size of the old one and also includes the opposite bank of the Arno for the first time.

1193 Consular regime replaced, and a Podestà installed, who was not allowed to come from Florence, and who represented the people's interests only for a limited term.

1215 The beginning of civil strife between rival supporters of the pope (Guelfs) and the Holy Roman Emperor (Ghibellines) over issues of temporal power and politics, fuelled by class warfare and family vendettas. The papal party is uppermost in Florence, and the city is at war with Ghibelline Pisa, Pistoia and Siena.

1238–50 The Ghibellines attain power.

1248 New town walls erected that define the limits of Florence until 1865. Florence is now one of Europe's richest banking and mercantile cities and the florin is the established currency of European trade.

1250–60 Regime of the Primo Popolo, supported by the Guelfs, and now including the merchant class.

1260–6 Ghibellines in power.

1267 onwards Guelfs in power.

1283 In the Secondo Popolo the Signoria (government) is appointed by the *arti* (guilds). The nobility, now a single party, the *parte guelfa*, is excluded from high political office; anyone who joins a guild can automatically be elected. The party of the nobility splits up into two opposing factions, the *neri* and the *bianchi* (Black Guelfs and White Guelfs).

1284 Work begins on a third city wall with 70 towers, 8km (5 miles) long (finished in 1333).

1289 Serfdom abolished.

1293 Strife between Guelfs and Ghibellines now an outright class war. The merchant Guelfs pass an ordinance excluding aristocratic Ghibellines from public office.

1294 Construction work commences on the new cathedral.

1299 Work begins on the Palazzo Vecchio.

1324 Only the really rich can now be elected to power; the less wealthy are gradually excluded from political office.

1339 Edward III of England defaults on massive debts incurred fighting the 100 Years' War. The two most powerful banking families, the Bardi and Peruzzi, go bankrupt and the Florentine economy is in crisis.

1348 The Black Death reduces the population of Florence from 100,000 to just 45,000.

1378 *Ciompi* uprising: the wool-carder guilds and all those denied a say in political life demand the right to be heard, but only manage to keep power for six weeks; dubious role played by the Medici.

1400–1 Competition to design new doors for the Baptistry announced. This event marks the beginning of the Renaissance.

1434 Cosimo il Vecchio (Cosimo the Elder) from the banking family of the Medici is called back from exile; he founds the Medici dynasty.

1439 Cosimo the Elder succeeds in having the Council of Ferrara transferred to Florence; the Byzantine Emperor John Paleologus VIII vainly asks for help against the Turkish threat.

1469–92 Cosimo's grandson, Lorenzo the Magnificent, is a wealthy Renaissance prince; Florence flourishes both economically and culturally.

1478 The Pazzi Conspiracy: Lorenzo's brother Giuliano is murdered.

1490 Death of Lorenzo, aged 44. His son, Piero, takes over.

1494–8 Charles VII of France invades Italy and Piero surrenders Florence to him. The Medicis are driven from the city by the outraged citizens. The Republic is taken over by the Dominican monk Savonarola, who is burnt at the stake in 1498.

1498–1512 Niccolò Machiavelli is head of chancery; Lorenzo's son Giovanni becomes a cardinal, and later Pope Leo X, and precipitates the collapse of the Republic.

1512–27 The Medicis rule Florence again.

1527–30 The sack of Rome by Charles V's troops, and the expulsion of Medici Pope Clement VII bring the Republic back to Florence briefly.

1530 Emperor Charles V captures Florence and installs Alessandro de' Medici as duke; the dynasty rules the city until 1737. Alessandro (1530–7); Cosimo I (1537–74); Francesco I (1574–87); Ferdinando I (1587–1609); Cosimo II (1609–21); Ferdinando II (1621–70); Cosimo III (1670–1723); Gian Gaston (1723–37) – the dynasty dies out.

1555 Capture of Siena.

1569 The title of Grand Duke is bestowed on the Medici dynasty.

1737–1859 After succession of Francesco of Lorraine, Tuscany becomes part of Austria and remains so with the exception of the Napoleonic Wars 1799–1815.

1848 After succession of Francesco of Lorraine, Tuscany becomes part of Austria and remains so except during the Napoleonic Wars 1799–1815.

1848 First Italian War of Independence; Tuscany is the vanguard of the uprising.

1860 Florence and Tuscany join the new United Kingdom of Italy.

1865–71 Florence is capital of Italy.

1887–1912 Tuscany remains economically buoyant, helped by textile production, and Florence becomes a haven for foreign poets and novelists.

1919 Mussolini founds the Fascist Party.

1940 Italy enters World War II.

1944 Retreating Germans destroy three of Florence's bridges, leaving only the Ponte Vecchio.

1946 Marshall Plan aid helps rebuild the Tuscan economy and Florence establishes itself as a centre of fashion.

1966 The River Arno floods (4 November), causing immense damage. Many works of art destroyed.

1988 Florentines vote for measures to exclude traffic from the historic city centre.

1993 The Uffizi Palace is severly damaged by a Mafia-placed bomb.

The Duomo

Preceding pages: view of Florence from the Piazzale Michelangelo

Sightseeing in style

The Baptistry of St John

Route 1

★★★ Piazza San Giovanni – ★★★ Piazza del Duomo (Cathedral Square)

The ★★★ **Piazza San Giovanni** and the ★★★ **Piazza del Duomo** still retain all their medieval splendour. The polychromatic marble used for the Baptistry, the Campanile and the Duomo creates a harmonious ensemble that still dominates the city skyline. The cathedral facade is currently being restored, amid some controversy; critics claim the colours are too bright and that the restored facades will not withstand air pollution.

★★★ Baptistry ❶

History of the building and its exterior

The exact history of the *Battistero di San Giovanni* (Baptistry of St John) is still uncertain. Its site on the outskirts of the Roman city, the borders of which were still valid during the period of its construction, point to the possibility of an earlier building from Roman times – according to legend, a temple consecrated to Mars, though other sources suggest a Roman governors' palace (1st century AD). Coin finds dating from the 4th and 5th centuries point to a former church on the site that was rebuilt around the beginning of the 11th century. Today's Baptistry was consecrated in the year 1059, but the building was only finally completed in the 13th century. The rectangular western apse was added in 1202; the attic floor is also 13th-century; and the graceful lantern roof dates from 1150. The octagonal central structure, a common design for Early Christian baptistries, was decorated in a style quite out of keeping with contemporary trends. This had its reasons: during the Investiture Controversy (the power struggle between the pope and the emperor) the trading city of Florence preferred to remain independent, and this meant that the 'imperial' Romanesque architectural style from the north (as manifested in the city-state of Pisa) was never actually adopted by Florence. The city took its architectural cue from Antiquity instead; the dichromatic marble exterior of the Baptistry and its formal combination of semicircles and right-angles are derived directly from it. The green bands of marble lend movement and perspective to the white marble-clad exterior, an effect disturbed somewhat by the horizontal stripes of the angle pilasters, which were added by cathedral architect Arnolfo di Cambio in the year 1296.

Despite all its architectural alterations the Baptistry was always considered to be a Roman structure; Dante (died 1321) believed this and so did Brunelleschi (died 1446). Since the Renaissance had such a strong and conscious affinity with Antiquity during the 15th century, the exterior of the Baptistry is referred to as 'Florentine Romanesque'. A similar architectural style is displayed by San Miniato al Monte (*see page 76*) and the Badia Fiesolana (*see page 77*), both of which were also built in the 11th century.

The three sets of gilded bronze doors on the Baptistry are internationally famous. The earliest, the South Door, is by Andrea Pisano (1330–6); it was cast in Venice and took him just six months to create. The 28 gilded compartments are surrounded by Gothic quatrefoil frames. In 20 panels the story of John the Baptist is recounted; the pictorial representations are completely separate from their surrounding medallions, emphasising the autonomy of the composition. The theological and cardinal virtues are represented below. The door-frame, with its plant motifs and figures, is the work of Vittorio Ghiberti (1452–62,

South Door: Beheading of John the Baptist

15

South Door: gilded bronze detail

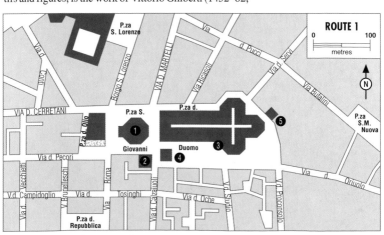

son of Lorenzo), and the bronze figures of the *Baptist*, the *Executioner*, and *Salome* above the portal are by Vincenzo Danti (1571).

North Door: frame decoration

The competition in 1401 for the North Door was won by Lorenzo Ghiberti, and it took him until 1424 to complete the work. The basis remained the same: 28 compartments, and the same medallions. Ghiberti made use of the form but filled it differently; his compositions have more freedom and movement to them, and are far more dynamic than those of Pisano – almost a century had elapsed. The two lower registers depict the Evangelists and Doctors of the Church. The chronological sequence of *Scenes from the life of Christ* begins on the third panel from the bottom of the left-hand door and continues towards the top, running left to right. The corners of the panels are decorated with bronze heads, one of which (fifth head from the top of the left door, middle band) is a self-portrait of Ghiberti. He also did the beautiful decoration of the frame. The bronze figures above, showing *John the Baptist preaching*, *the Levite*, and *the Pharisee* are by Francesco Rustici (1506–11).

Not far from the portal a pillar, erected in 1384, stands as a reminder of a legend: an elm tree is said to have blossomed on this spot on 26 January 429, while the body of St Zenobius was being carried by. For the East Door of the Baptistry, which faces the Duomo, Lorenzo Ghiberti created what Michelangelo is said to have termed the ★★**Gates of Paradise** (1425–52), a complete contrast to the South Door and his own North Door. It has 10 separate, large-format compartments, simple and rectangular, no longer restricted to a Gothic frame, and each door is surrounded once again by continuous gilded panels. The use of perspective here is of great importance: scenes with low relief extend far into the background, and the com-

The Gates of Paradise

position is strikingly natural. The panels show scenes from the Old Testament; the framing contains a portrait of Ghiberti himself, looking rather mischievous [11].

Above the door is the sculptural group of the *Baptism of Christ*. *John the Baptist* and *Jesus* are by Andrea Sansovino (1502), and the *Angel* was added by Vincenzo Spinazzi in 1792.

Subjects (diagram)

1 *The Creation and Expulsion from Paradise*
2 *Cain and Abel*
3 *Noah's sacrifice and drunkenness*
4 *Abraham and the Angels and the Sacrifice of Isaac*
5 *Esau and Jacob*
6 *Joseph sold into Egypt and recognised by his brothers*
7 *Moses receiving the stone tablets*
8 *The Fall of Jericho*
9 *Saul's Battle with the Philistines; David defeats Goliath*
10 *Solomon and the Queen of Sheba*

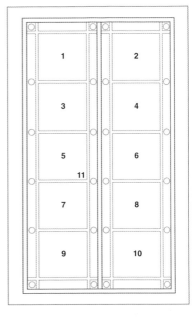

Interior

The Baptistry's interior is designed in two orders: the lower one has huge granite columns from a Roman building, with gilded Corinthian capitals, and the upper one has a gallery with divided windows above a cornice. The apse and the three portals are emphasised by double pillars and round arches extending the entire height of the walls.

The floor (12th–13th century) is decorated with mosaics showing geometrical motifs and also the 12 signs of the zodiac; the font that once stood at the centre (Dante was christened here) fell victim to the liturgical reform of the 16th century. On the right of the apse, between two columns, is the tomb of Antipope John XXIII (died 1419 in Florence) by Donatello, assisted by Michelozzo.

Donatello's famous wood sculpture of ★★ **St Mary Magdalen**, which used to stand to the left of the apse, can now be admired in the Museo dell'Opera del Duomo. The mosaics on the apse, frieze and dome were started in 1226, and the work continued until the beginning of the 14th century. Byzantine mosaicists were brought from Venice to do the work, and they passed on their skills to the local artists.

Most striking of all is the *Last Judgement* with the huge figure of Christ, surrounded on three sides of the octagon with the medieval representation of hell. The remaining five sides of the octagon are divided into four

Last Judgement mosaic

Relaxing in the Piazza

bands, showing the story of John the Baptist, the story of Genesis (Creation and Flood), the story of Christ, and the story of Joseph. The inner band showing the story of Christ depicts the creator and the heavenly host, and vines – symbols of heavenly paradise – growing up towards the lantern above. The colour of the entire mosaic in the vault changes subtly from the sombre tones of the Last Judgement to the bright gold of Heaven, opening up the prospect of paradise.

On the corner of the Piazza San Giovanni and the Via de' Calzaiuoli is the headquarters of a charitable institution founded in the 13th century, the **Loggia del Bigallo** . The present building was constructed between 1351 and 1358, and its magnificent loggia with its marble decor is typical of the International Gothic style of the 14th century. The exhibits in the small museum inside include the first known pictorial representation of Florence (1345), on an icon of unknown origin and also a painted crucifix (1225–35), also by an unknown master, one of the earliest examples of panel painting in Florence (access only by prior appointment with the Florence building authority *Soprintendenza per i Beni Artistichi*).

The Duomo

★★★ *Duomo Santa Maria del Fiore*

(open daily: 10am–5.30pm).
History of the cathedral
After the city limits were extended in 1284 when construction work began on the third city wall, the Florentines decided that their city, which had become so powerful, needed something more representative than just the Baptistry. The new cathedral was begun after long deliberation in 1294, with the aim of outdoing such rival cities as Pisa, Siena and Orvieto – so the relevant dimensions were decided on. Master builder Arnolfo di Cambio was awarded the contract, and the foundation stone was laid on 8 September 1296. The site was the area around the cathedral of Santa Reparata, opposite the Baptistry, which because of slow progress on the project actually remained standing until 1375. The new cathedral was renamed Santa Maria del Fiore.

Construction work first came to a standstill in 1310 when Arnolfo died. It was continued only in 1334, when Giotto was hired, but he concentrated first and foremost on his Campanile. Work stopped yet again after his death in 1337. Then the building work continued with a new design 20 years later, and in 1367 the final shape of the cathedral was decided. In 1378 the centre nave was given its vault, followed by the side aisles in 1380, and the choir section was completed by 1421. Filippo Brunelleschi had already won the competition for the dome in 1418, and his revolutionary construction was ready in 1436. On 25

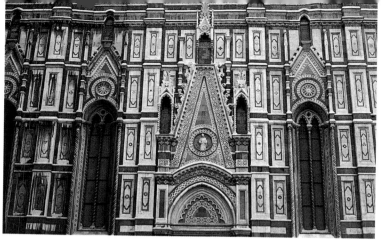

The flank of the Duomo

March that year – the Florentine New Year – Pope Eugene IV consecrated the cathedral, even though the lantern was not finally completed until 1461. No-one could make a decision on what sort of facade the cathedral should have for years (the Museo dell'Opera del Duomo contains models of several of the versions suggested). It was only in the 19th century that a neo-Gothic facade by De Fabris (1871–87) was finally decided on, but this solution rather jars with the original architectural ideals involved.

19

Exterior

The huge dimensions of the structure as a whole are most impressive. The formal language, borrowed from Antiquity, of semicircles and right-angles, of which the Baptistry (11th-century) is the earliest example, was retained by the Florentines right across to the apse of the Duomo, at the other end of this huge collection of buildings; the breaks in style during the 15th century, though visible, have little effect on the architectural unity of the whole.

The 19th-century facade jars with the forms borrowed from Antiquity; its many small patterns on the horizontal and vertical sections as well as on its triangular gable are rather uncomfortable, and the right-angles at the top of the gable seem to have been just placed there. It was on the right-hand side of the Duomo that Giotto built his ★★ **Campanile** ❹ (ascent in summer 9am–7.30pm, in winter 9am–5.30pm).

Giotto's Campanile

This bell-tower was originally supposed to have been 100m (330ft) high, but Giotto's plans were altered after his death in 1337. The only section designed by him is the lowest storey, with the portal that was added later. The ★ **bas-reliefs** (their originals are in the Museo dell'Opera del Duomo) illustrate the Creation of Man, and the Arts and Industries. They are the work of Andrea Pisano; the cycle begins on the left-hand side of the east face.

Rhomboid medallions

The second storey, with its rhomboid medallions, was added by Pisano after Giotto's death, and shows the Planets (Baptistry side), the Virtues (south side), the Liberal Arts (west side) and the Sacraments (north side), executed by pupils of Pisano according to his original designs. It was Pisano who added the third storey too; he designed it vertically, with embrasures in the middle. Two rows of niches run horizontally, one containing casts of statues. Pisano died in 1348, and it was Francesco Talenti who completed the Campanile (1350–9). He added two more storeys, each with a pair of double-mullioned windows and playful Gothic ornamentation, and crowned his work with the belfry, which is just as high as the two storeys beneath it, its triple-mullioned openings leading up to the cornice above.

Even though it was designed by three different architects, the Campanile is still a masterpiece of elegance: the horizontal bands at the base lend extra strength to the soaring tendency of the windowed storeys – Pisano's niche storeys remain caught between the two, rather indecisively. The use of pink marble as a third colour alongside the green and white creates an impression of lightness, as does Giotto's idea of framing the tower with octagonal corner buttresses and then lightening it further up by using large Gothic windows – despite the height of almost 85m (275ft) and the fact that the walls are over 3m (10ft) thick. The Campanile in Florence is widely considered to be the finest in all Italy.

View from the Campanile towards the Palazzo Vecchio…

…and the Duomo

On the southern side of the Duomo, right next to the Campanile, the change of plan in 1367 has left its traces: the outer structure of the first bay actually dates from the earliest plan by Arnolfo di Cambio. The playful way in which it has been subdivided, with its narrow windows, small surfaces and jutting pilasters, lends it a touch of International Gothic and gives one an idea of Arnolfo's original plan for the cathedral's exterior. The change of plan in 1367, which determined four nave bays instead of three and also higher walls, disturbed the rhythmic refinement of the first version; from the second bay onwards the structuring is quite different, only allowing room for a single large window. The two different structures are unified, however, by the band of green and white marble running below the ledge. The Porta dei Canonici (Canons' Gate) [a] in the fourth bay (*see ground-plan, page 22*) dates from before 1400, and its fine sculptured decoration was added in 1402.

The exterior of the choir section should be seen as a cleverly structured architectural mass, from the lantern on the cupola all the way down to street-level. The enormous weight of the world-famous cupola is cleverly diffused via a series of carefully-positioned structural components: the trefoil choir with its three large apses, and the two sacristies. The cupola has two concentric shells, the outer one being thinner than the inner one. Brunelleschi, who designed the dome, perfected the rhythm of the choir end by placing the four decorative little exedrae, with their niches and red roofs, around the octagonal drum between the three domed tribunes housing the choir chapels.

Each of the tribunes was originally to have been decorated with four statues of the Apostles by Michelangelo, making a total of 12, but he did not actually carry out the work. This was possibly because he was too critical: he referred to the balcony at the base of the cupola, covering the brickwork on the southeast side (1508–12), as a 'crickets' cage' – and it was never completed.

Brunelleschi's cupola

The alteration in the plans of 1367 aimed at building a cupola that would put those of Pisa and Siena in the shade and represent the sheer might of the city-state of Florence. The nave, the crossing and the octagonal drum were completed by 1412–3; the construction of the dome itself, however, posed several structural problems. Filippo Brunelleschi, who had won the competition for the commission in 1418, promised to construct the huge cupola – which only starts 50m (160ft) above the ground – in a series of rings without the need for a wooden supporting frame. On each of the eight sides, a master worked with a team of nine masons to construct the double-shelled dome. Brunelleschi kept an eye on the manufacture of the tiles and the composition of the mortar, organised the distribution of bread and wine for the workers, and also invented several new pieces of apparatus during construction of the dome (some of which can be seen in the Museo dell'Opera del Duomo).

21

Under the suspicious gaze of his contemporaries, Brunelleschi's dome grew and grew. It was finally completed in 1436. Brunelleschi also designed the lantern that crowns it, but did not live to see its completion. It was only put into position in 1461. For the eight buttresses supporting the 19-m (60-ft) high temple with its eight narrow windows, Brunelleschi created decorative scrolls, which point the way towards baroque – and are also similar to the scrolls on the facade of Santa Maria Novella (1458) by Leon Battista Alberti.

Decorative scroll

The entire structure was finally crowned in 1472 by Verrocchio's bronze ball and cross, thus finally reaching its proud height of 107m (350ft). The best view of the edifice as a whole can be obtained from just in front of the **Museo dell'Opera del Duomo ❺**.

The stroll around the outside of the Duomo then leads to the north face, and the Porta della Mandorla **[b]**; this was built at the same time as the nave (1391–5), and its decorative sculpture was added in the early 15th century.

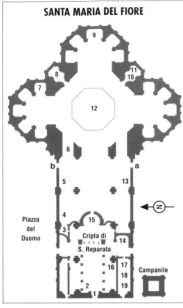

SANTA MARIA DEL FIORE

9

8
11
10
7

12

6

b   a

5   13

←(z)→

4   15

Piazza
del   3
Duomo   Cripta di   14
S. Reparata

16 17
18   Campanile
2   19

1

The entire portal is a masterpiece of International Gothic. Several artists contributed to it: in the gable is an *Assumption of the Virgin* (1414–21) in a mandorla by Nanni di Banco, where Mary can be seen handing her girdle to Doubting Thomas. The natural gestures here already herald the Renaissance (Mary's girdle is the most important item in the cathedral treasure of Prato, *see page 80*).

Interior of Santa Maria del Fiore
The three-aisled cruciform basilica is lit by high Gothic windows in the side-aisles of the second, third and fourth bays; the alteration made to the plans in 1367 did not retain the finer structuring by Arnolfo, the first architect, and his windows in the first bay have now been filled in and can only be admired from outside. The vault of the nave and the octagonal drum beneath the dome. The clear formal language of this interior points the way towards the Renaissance, but the decorative elements are still playful Gothic – a combination characteristic of Florentine art.

The stained-glass windows in the nave date from when the cathedral was built and show *Scenes from the Life of the Virgin* by Donatello, Paolo Uccello, Andrea del Castagno and Lorenzo Ghiberti, who also did the three round windows. The floor (1526–1660) was based on designs by Baccio d'Agnolo and Francesco da Sangallo.

1 The most distinctive feature of the interior is the large astronomical clock beneath the mosaic portraying the *Coronation of the Virgin* (early 14th-century); the clock's face with its four heads of the prophets was painted by Paolo Uccello in 1443. The clock uses the *hora italica* method of counting the hours; the last hour of the day ends at sunset or Ave Maria. The system was used in Italy until the 18th century.

2 Tomb of Antonio d'Orso, Bishop of Florence (died 1321), a good but incomplete work by the Sienese sculptor Tino di Camaino.

3 Equestrian memorial to *condottiere* (soldier of fortune) Noccolò da Tolentino by Andrea del Castagno (1456); a variation on No 4 (below) by Paolo Uccello.

4 Equestrian memorial to *condottiere* John Hawkwood by Paolo Uccello (1436). This is a fresco giving the illusion of sculpture; newly-discovered perspective can be seen in the rendition of the plinth.

5 *Dante e suoi mondi* (Dante and His Worlds) by Domenico di Michelino (1465). Florence celebrated the 200th anniversary of the poet's birth; he can be seen holding an open copy of his *Divina Commedia*. The

*One of the many
interior sculptures*

city panorama shows the cathedral's cupola still under construction. Dante's outstretched hand points at the three worlds of his *Commedia*: *Inferno* on the left, *Purgatorio* in the background, and above it *Paradiso*.

6 Entrance for ascent of the dome (weekdays 10am–5.30pm). The 463 steps here provide a good view of the inner structure of the double-shelled cupola; the inner shell is 4m (13ft) thick, the outer one only 80cm (2.5ft). The panorama of the city from the top of the dome is most rewarding.

Aisle detail

7 ★★ *Pietà* by Michelangelo (c 1550); the original is in the Museo dell'Opera del Duomo.

8 *Risurrezione* (Resurrection) by Luca della Robbia (1442–5); the portal leads to the New (or North) Sacristy. *(See Ascenzione below.)*

9 Main altar with bronze shrine to the city's other patron saint, St Zenobius, by Lorenzo Ghiberti, executed at the same time as the Baptistry's Doors of Paradise (1432–42).

10 *Ascenzione* (Ascension) by Luca della Robbia (c 1450); the portal leads into the Old (or South) Sacristy *(See Risurrezione above.)*

11 *Angelo portacandelabro* (Angel with Candelabra) by Luca della Robbia.

12 Crossing with dome. A good view here of the trefoil choir section with the three choir chapels. There is a fine view of the recently restored dome fresco of the *Last Judgement* by Vasari (1572–4) 50m (160ft) up, completed by Zuccari (1578–9). The three choir chapels and the drum are all octagonal, echoing the ground-plan of the Baptistry. The eight pilasters of the crossing contain statues of the Apostles by Ammannati (1565); *St James* is thought to be an early work by Jacopo Sansovino (1511–18).

23

Vasari's Last Judgement in the dome

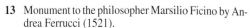

13 Monument to the philosopher Marsilio Ficino by Andrea Ferrucci (1521).

14 *San Bartolomeo in trono* (St Bartholomew Enthroned) by Rossello di Jacopo Franchi (1408).

15 Excavations of the former building on the site, Santa Reparata (opening hours: weekdays 10am–5.30pm). Santa Reparta was discovered in 1966, and in 1972 Brunelleschi's coffin was also unearthed. The ruins of this church, which was demolished in 1375, show a three-aisled basilica ground-plan with raised choir and crypt. Foundations thought to be those of a far earlier structure (4th–5th-century) were also discovered. There are several archaeological exhibits and also remains of mosaics.

16 Gothic stoup (c 1380); the original is in the Museo dell'Opera del Duomo.

17 Bust of Giotto by Benedetto da Maiano (1490).

18 The prophet Daniel, attributed to Donatello (c 1408).

19 Bust of Fillipo Brunelleschi by his pupil Andrea Cavalcanti (1447).

After this tour of the interior it is a good idea to take a look back inside the cathedral from the central portal: the gilt-framed panels on the first two pillars are particularly striking in the soft evening light: on the left nave pillar, *St Zenobius* by Giovanni del Biondo (1375–80) and on the right pillar *St Anthony*, prior of San Marco and Archbishop of Florence, painted by Poppi (1589).

Museo dell'Opera del Duomo

The building at No 9, Piazza del Duomo, opposite the cathedral's main apse, has been used for maintenance purposes since the 15th century, and since 1891 has housed the ★★ **Museo dell'Opera del Duomo** ❺, the Cathedral Museum (weekdays in summer 9am–7.30pm, in winter 9am–6pm). It contains superb works of art taken from the Duomo, Baptistry and Campanile.

The dramatic story of the cathedral facade can be relived on the ground floor. A contemporary sketch illustrates the facade by Arnolfo di Cambio, the cathedral's first architect, which was torn down in 1588. The figures planned by Arnolfo as decoration – of uncertain origin – are also visible. The sculpture on display in the museum consists mostly of statues and figures created to adorn the Duomo, Baptistry and Campanile, and so the best sculptors of Florence, active in the 14th and 15th centuries, are represented: Andrea Pisano, Filippo Brunelleschi, Lorenzo Ghiberti, Donatello, Nanni di Banco and Luca della Robbia.

The Sale Brunelleschi contain a wooden model of his masterpiece, the cupola, and also several of his architectural inventions. The various models submitted for the facade competition in the 16th century are on display in a room of their own; none was ever realised.

The half-landing on the way to the upper floor was chosen for one of the most famous pieces of sculpture in the world: Michelangelo's ★★ **Pietà**, which was brought here from the cathedral in 1981. Michelangelo, who started the work in Rome around the year 1550 when he was roughly 75, and intended it for his own tomb, gave it to his pupil Tiberio Calcagni as a present because the Christ figure had a broken leg; Calcagni had it improved. In 1722 the *Pietà* found its way into Florence Cathedral. Despite restoration, it is one of the most impressive sculpture groups in the history of art; the figure of the mourning Joseph of Arimathea (or possibly, Nicodemus) is a self-portrait.

The upper floor of the museum is dominated by the two ★★ **Cantorie** (singing galleries) by Donatello (1433–9) and Luca della Robbia (1432–8), which used to stand above the two sacristy doors in the Duomo. In the hall next door, the original hexagonal bas-reliefs from the lowest storey of the Campanile can be admired; the lower row is by Giotto, the upper by Andrea Pisano. The corridor then leads into a room containing the distinctive silver altar of St John the Baptist. It was originally in the Baptistry, and naturally no expense was spared during its construction – the work lasted from 1366 to 1480. Goldsmiths were as native to Florence as cloth merchants, and the silver-gilt work here is proof of it, as are the bronze doors of the Baptistry. The altar is Gothic, and the statuette of the Baptist in the centre niche at the front was added by Michelozzo. The reliefs showing scenes from the life of St John are almost too large for their frames. The eight scenes on the front of the altar and the two on each of its sides are the work of various artists. The *Decollazione* (Beheading of the Baptist) by Andrea del Verrocchio (1477–80) on the right-hand side is very realistically done.

Cantorie by Donatello

Michelangelo's Pietà

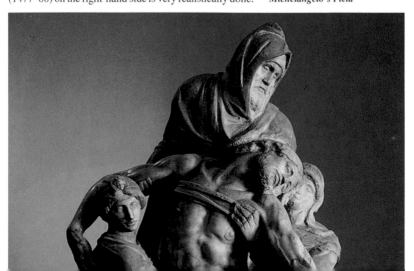

Route 2

★★★ **Piazza della Signoria** – ★★ **Palazzo Vecchio** –
★★★ **Uffizi** – ★ **Santi Apostoli** – ★ **Santa Trinità**–
★★ **Palazzo Rucellai** – **San Gaetano** – **Santa Maria**
Maggiore – **Piazza San Giovanni**

Piazza della Signoria

From 1300 onwards, the ★★★ **Piazza della Signoria** became the centre of secular power in Florence. Dante, too,
resided for two months as a representative of the people
in the new government building, the Palazzo della Signoria, which was started here in 1299. As affirmation of
their power, the ruling Guelfs built it in an area formerly
occupied by Ghibelline families, and the building has been
referred to as the Palazzo Vecchio (Old Palace) ever since
the Medici moved into the Palazzo Pitti in 1559. Excavations in the piazza have revealed traces of the former
Ghibelline structures, as well as Roman and prehistoric
remains. After a great deal of discussion as to what to do
about the excavations, it was finally decided to fill in the
square again.

The huge Loggia della Signoria – which had its name
changed to the **Loggia dei Lanzi** in 1530 because of German Emperor Charles V's lancers *(lanzichenecchi)* who
were stationed here as a bodyguard for Cosimo I – forms
a very distinctive part of the piazza, and was built between
1376 and 1382. It was designed for ceremonial and official events for the *signoria* and the townspeople; the harmonious round arches and the artistically shaped pillars
they rest on represent a total rejection of the International

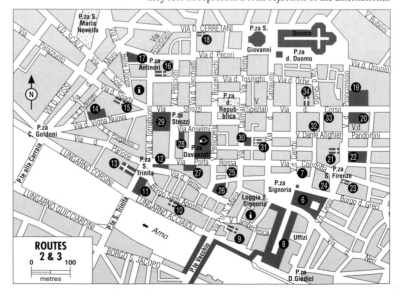

ROUTES
2 & 3
0   100
metres

Loggia dei Lanzi

Gothic style a whole generation before Brunelleschi. The medallions display the common Florentine mixture of semicircles and corners; the statues in the hall are antique and Renaissance, and the most famous ones are at the front: *Perseus* by Benvenuto Cellini (1553) is left of the staircase, and Giambologna's *Rape of the Sabine* (1583) stands to the right.

27

Bartolomeo Ammannati's Fountain of Neptune (1575) and Giambologna's equestrian statue of Cosimo I (1594) came a lot later. It was Cosimo I who got Michelangelo to start thinking about a possible extension of the piazza. For financial reasons it retained its irregular shape, and with its exhibition of sculptures along the palazzo facade and the right-angled loggia, it resembles nothing more than a well-structured open-air museum.

The main theme here – directly derived from the fierce pride of the city-state – is 'liberty': the word *libertas* appears twice in the coat-of-arms under the projecting battlements; Donatello's *Lion (Marzocco)*, which dates from 1420 (a copy: the original is in the Bargello), can be seen holding the city's fleur-de-lys in its paw; alongside it is Donatello's group *Judith and Holofernes* (1455–60); in front of the portal, Michelangelo's *David* (1504) (a copy: the original is in the Accademia); and next to that is *Hercules and Nessos* (1533) by Bandinelli. The many large and small lions on the loggia all suit the general picture; the city was finally given its own real lions at the end of the 18th century.

Hercules and Nessos

★★ *Palazzo Vecchio* ❻

Alongside the cathedral, this is Florence's most famous landmark. Cathedral architect Arnolfo di Cambio began work on this edifice in 1299, and most of it, including the 94-m (300-ft) high tower, was completed by the year 1314; extension work then followed in 1343, 1495, 1511,

Palazzo Vecchio

1540–3 (new interior), 1549–55 and 1588–92. The Italian parliament met here between 1865 and 1871 when Florence was the capital of reunified Italy; today it is the mayor's official residence, and the majestic inner rooms are used for exhibitions and concerts. The only room that provides a good idea of what most of these inner chambers must have been like originally is the *Sala d'Arme* (Weapons Hall); the entrance to this unpretentious vaulted room, set aside for special exhibitions, is on the north side of the building.

The building looks as defensive as ever, although in medieval times there was a wall the height of a man running all the way round. The distinctly Florentine divided windows only begin very high up the facade. The mighty battlemented gallery juts out, and the tower grows out of it to a height of 94m (300ft); for the bell-tower a special storey supported by four pillars was added. The battlements and tower of the Bargello (*see page 39*), which was built somewhat earlier, are modest by comparison.

Palazzo Vecchio: in the Cortille

Courtyard and Interior

(weekdays except Saturday 9am–7pm, Sunday and public holidays 8am–1pm). The inner courtyard that one enters first was laid out by Michelozzo, who 'modernised' it between 1439 and 1454. It received its present-day decoration on the occasion of the lavish wedding of Francesco de' Medici and Joanna of Austria in 1565. Giorgio Vasari had the pillars refurbished with stucco and gold, and the ceilings painted in Pompeiian style. The walls were decorated with *vedute* of Austrian cities – much to the surprise of the bride, apparently. The winged goblin holding a dolphin, on top of the fountain in the centre of the courtyard, is a copy of a work by Andrea del Verrocchio (1476).

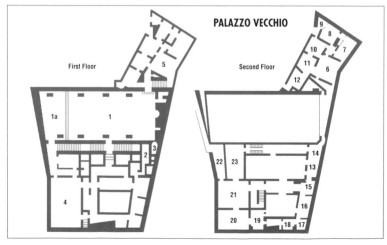

Tapestry: Joseph and Potiphar's Wife in the Sala dei Dugento

Quartieri monumentali

After the Medicis finally established autocratic rule in 1537, Cosimo I commissioned art critic, painter and architect Giorgio Vasari to refurbish the palace interior. Visiting depends on various factors such as special exhibitions or restoration work, and sometimes rooms are used by the municipal administration.

29

1 **Salone dei Cinquecento**. Modelled after the Doge's Palace in Venice, this large salon was built in 1494, and Vasari transformed it in 1563–5 when the present decoration was carried out in honour of Cosimo I. Vasari and his pupils glorify the Medici family and the city's history in the panels of the gilt coffered ceiling; this huge undertaking (there are 39 paintings on the ceiling alone) was the result of just three days' conversation between Vasari and Prince Francesco. Their dialogues were published as *Ragionamenti* and are of documentary value. The magnificent *Udienza* (audience area) [a] is a raised tribuna, and is distinctive for its neoclassical decor, marble intarsia and statues of members of the Medici family. Among the sculptures here is Michelangelo's *Victory* (second from the left opposite the entrance).

Ceiling detail in the Studiolo di Francesco I

2 **Studiolo di Francesco I**. This tiny study, with its barrel vault, was decorated in the Florentine Mannerist style by the Vasari school (c 1570).

3 **Tesoretto**. A small staircase leads to the private study of Grand Duke Cosimo I.

4 **Sala dei Dugento**. The name is derived from the council of 200 persons who met here in 1441; Giuliano and Benedetto da Maiano built the hall between 1475 and 1480. The ★ **coffered ceiling** has been attributed to Michelozzo.

5 Sala di Leone X. The frescoes here, painted in 1560, are devoted to the Medici pope and scenes from his life. Michelangelo and Leonardo da Vinci can both be seen in the painting illustrating the *Appointment of the 21 Cardinals*, and on the picture of Florence the church of San Pietro Scheraggio can be seen; it was pulled down to make way for the Uffizi. The other rooms here are used by the municipal administration; on the lower half-landing on the way up to the second floor there is a 16th-century fresco of the piazza showing the defensive wall that ran in front of the palazzo.

6 Sala degli Elementi. Vasari decorated the ceiling of this room – which was built by Giovanni Battista del Tasso – with complicated allegories of the four elements: earth, air, fire and water.

7–12 The neighbouring rooms are named after the mythological themes illustrated in their paintings: the Loggiato di Saturno (Saturn) [7], Sala di Ercole (Hercules) [8], Terrazzo di Giunone (Juno) [9], containing the original of Verrocchio's winged goblin (copy on the fountain in the courtyard), Sala di Giove (Jupiter) [10] with two marvellous cabinets in pietra-dura, Sala di Cibele (Cybele) [11] with its original floor and wooden cabinets and the Sala di Cerere (Ceres) [12].

Fresco in the Chapel of Eleonora of Toledo

13–18 Quartiere di Eleonora di Toledo. Vasari refashioned these apartments for the wife of Cosimo I in 1562. The Camera Verde (Green Room) [13] provides access to a tiny secret chamber in the outer wall. The Cappella [14] is adorned with frescoes by Agnolo Bronzino (1564). The following rooms were illustrated with allegories of the Female Virtues: Camera delle Sabine [15], Camera di Ester [16], formerly a dining-room, Camera di Penelope [17], a study, and Camera di Gualdrada (the Grand Duchess's bedchamber) [18].

19 Cappella della Signoria. Frescoes are by Ridolfo del Ghirlandaio (1514); altarpiece is by his pupil Mariano da Pescia.

20 Sala dell'Udienza. The magnificent gilt ceiling and the intarsia work on the doors leading to the Sala dei Gigli, with the figures of Dante and Petrarch (c 1480), are the work of Giuliano da Maiano and his assistants. The marble portal leading to the chapel dates from the final days of the Republic (1529).

21 Sala dei Gigli. The golden lilies on a white background are a reminder of the Republic's futile alliance with France against the German emperor. The portal and the ceiling are by the Maiano work-

Golden lilies in the Sala dei Gigli

shop. Heraldic lions can be seen beneath the ceiling right round the room; the fresco showing St Zenobius is by Domenico Ghirlandaio (1481–5). Donatello's bronze statue of ★ *Judith and Holofernes* is also on display here.

22 **Cancelleria**. This room was used as an office by Niccolò Machiavelli; his portrait and bust are by Santo di Tito.

23 **Guardaroba**. The wooden cupboards are adorned with historic maps; the 53 panels are the work of Stefano Buonsignori (1575–84) and before him Ignazio Danti (1563–75), who also created the huge map of the world in the middle of the room.

The Sala dei Gigli also provides access to the tower. Via the Ballatoio, the walk along the battlements, one can reach the Sala delle Bandiere where legal sentences were pronounced, and also the *Alberghettino* (little inn), which was used to house state prisoners, including Cosimo the Elder before his exile (1433) and also Savonarola (8 April–22 May 1498). The tower is closed to visitors at present.

On the way to the exit, there is a fine Musical Instrument Museum (admission only after prior application) on the mezzanine floor, containing instruments by the violin-makers Amati, Stradivari and Guarneri, as well as historic hurdy-gurdies, woodwind and brass instruments.

Anyone keen on contemporary Italian art should visit house No 5 on the Piazza della Signoria, which contains the **Alberto della Ragione collection** ❼ (opening hours weekdays except Tuesday 9am–2pm, Sunday and public holidays 8am–1pm). Owned by the city, this gallery contains work by Marino Marini, Giorgio Morandi, Carlo Levi, Renato Guttuso and Emilio Vedova.

The Medici family ruled from the Palazzo Vecchio as absolute monarchs from 1531 onwards, and when they moved into the building the municipal authorities were forced to leave. Giorgio Vasari built a new home for them: the long, U-shaped **Uffizi Palace** ❽ (1560–70). He designed two storeys in Renaissance style, supported by Doric colonnades and an attic floor in between, and decorated the whole with a combination of rounded arches, triangles and rectangles.

The Uffizi Palace

The building formed a contrast to the Palazzo Vecchio next door, but a passageway connecting the Uffizi with the palazzo was built on the first floor, and from 1565 a corridor was constructed that led from the Uffizi across the Ponte Vecchio to the Palazzo Pitti, home of the ruling family. This was the **Corridoio Vasariano** (Vasari Corridor). Architecturally unique, this corridor today contains what is probably the largest collection of self-portraits in the world, which unfortunately may no longer be seen; after

Corridoio Vasariano and the Ponte Vecchio

Uffizi Gallery corridors

Leonardo at the Uffizi

the 1993 bomb attack on the Uffizi, the corridor has been closed indefinitely.

The successor of Cosimo I, Grand Duke Francesco I, ordered Vasari's successor Bernardo Buontalenti to convert the open loggia of the administrative building into rooms for the Medici family's art collections; the loggia thus became a *galleria* enclosed in glass in 1580, and today's expression 'art gallery' is derived from it. The Medici family housed its entire art collection there, and bequeathed it to the city of Florence in 1737.

Today the Uffizi building houses the remains of the church which had to be pulled down to make way for it, San Pietro Scheraggio (slightly damaged by the 1993 bomb, the church should be restored by 1995), as well as the Gabinetto dei Disegni e delle Stampe (Prints and Drawings Collection) – one of the finest collections in the world, and particularly rich in Renaissance and Mannerist works. The upper floor is devoted to the ★★★ **Galleria degli Uffizi**, the most important collection of paintings in Italy and one of the great art collections of the world (Tuesday–Saturday 9am–7pm, Sunday and public holidays 9am–1pm). Before visiting it, a brief stroll to get your bearings is recommended; there are fine views across the roofs of the city and of the other bank of the Arno. The corridors themselves are decorated with paintings, tapestries and antique statues.

The bomb attack on the Uffizi in 1993 closed half the gallery for a period, but by the end of 1994 over 85 percent of the works were once again on display. The remainder will be ready in 1995–6.

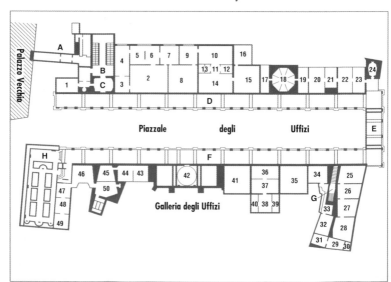

A Corridor leading to Palazzo Vecchio
B Administrative offices
C Vestibule containing statues of Roman emperors Julius Caesar, Augustus and Hadrian
D East Corridor. The painted ceiling (late 16th-century grotesque) features mythological scenes, landscapes and decorative motifs. Along the walls: Flemish tapestries, and also 16th-century Florentine cycle depicting the Twelve Months of the Year. The corridor also contains antique statues, sarcophagi and steles
E South Corridor. The ceiling here (17th-century grotesque) displays historical, religious and allegorical motifs. Fine antique sculpture, and a magnificent view of Florence
F West Corridor. The painted ceiling here is a continuation of the one in the South Corridor. The 16th-century tapestries here are from Florentine workshops (Passion cycle) and also Flemish (The Story of James; various battle scenes). Antique sculptures are found along the corridor.
G Staircase leading to the Corridoio Vasariano
H Terrace, bar, WC

The collection of paintings in the Uffizi contains unique masterpieces that provide an excellent general impression of Tuscan painting and of the way in which it freed itself from Byzantine severity and formality. This is particularly evident in the first halls, which contain works by Cimabue, Duccio, Giotto, Simone Martini, Ambrogio and Pietro Lorenzetti, Taddeo Gaddi, Bernardo Daddi, Andreo Orcagna, Gentile da Fabriano, Paolo Uccello, Beato Angelico, Domenico Veneziano, Masaccio, Piero della Francesca, Filippo Lippi, Benozzo Gozzoli, Antonio and Piero Pollaiuolo – the list can only provide a hint of what should be seen here.

Madonna and Child by Taddeo Gaddi

Primavera by Botticelli

Room 10 onward contains the full magnificence of Renaissance art, with works by Sandro Botticelli (including *Primavera* and the *Birth of Venus*), Filippino Lippi, Domenico Ghirlandaio, Luca Signorelli, Lorenzo di Credi, Verrocchio, and Leonardo da Vinci; these are interspersed with works of the Flemish school by Hans Memling, Rogier van der Weyden and also Hugo van der Goes, whose triptych of the *Adoration of the Shepherds*, commissioned by the Medici agent in Bruges, Portinari, had an important influence on contemporary Florentine artists. Room 17 contains antique sculptures and also paintings by Andrea Mantegna; and Room 18 contains the famous *Medici Venus*, a 4th-century Greek statue.

Central Italian painters (Room 19) and Venetian artists of the 15th and 16th centuries (Room 21) can be found on either side of the German masters Albrecht Dürer,

Michelangelo's Doni Holy Family

Lukas Cranach and Hans von Kulmbach in Room 20, and German painting is again represented by Hans Holbein and Albrecht Altdorfer in Room 22, alongside works by Bellini, Carpaccio, Giorgione and Cima da Conegliano. Room 23, at the very end of the East Corridor, contains works by painters from Emilia and Lombardy (Correggio and Sodoma) and also from Flanders.

After indulging briefly in the superb view of the other bank of the Arno from the South Corridor, Room 25 and the ones that follow it contain works by the greatest names in the history of Tuscan painting: Raphael, Andrea del Sarto, Rosso Fiorentino, and Michelangelo. Room 28 has several superb works by the Venetian artist Titian, Room 29 contains paintings by Parmigiano, from Parma, and the Emilian school is represented in Rooms 30 and 31. Room 32 has works by the Venetians Sebastiano del Piombo, Paris Bordone and Lorenzo Lotto; and Rooms 34 and 35 contain Venetian masterpieces by Paolo Veronese and Jacopo Tintoretto. Room 41 is dedicated to the work of Netherlands painter Peter Paul Rubens; the rooms that follow, containing works by Rembrandt, Carracci and Caravaggio and also several 18th-century French and Italian paintings, are being restructured; major names here include Canaletto, Francesco Guardi, Pietro Longhi, Rosalba Carriera and Antoine Watteau.

During the 19th century, the niches along Vasari's arcades were filled by rather unsuccessful statues representing leading national figures. Between those of goldsmith and sculptor Benvenuto Cellini and Guido of Arezzo, inventor of the musical staff, the Via Lambertesca leads off to the right. Even on the most crowded days at the Uffizi, this little medieval alley is usually an oasis of calm. Just before the end of it, through an archway before the last house to the left, is **Santo Stefano al Ponte** ❾. The

Andrea del Sarto: Young Girl Reading Petrarch

medieval city, with its churches and towers, grew up along this small stretch of land between the Roman wall and the Arno, and the facade of Santo Stefano still bears traces of Florentine Romanesque (*see page 83*), though the building as a whole was restored by Ferdinand Tacca in the 17th century. The interior, which is used for concerts today, contains Tacca's distinctive ★ **bronze altar frontal** of the *Stoning of St Stephen*. The ★ **altar steps** (1574) at the east end, a Mannerist work by Buontalenti, are also worthy of note; the clever use of perspective here is fascinating. (At the time of going to press, the Via Lambertesca was closed due to the 1993 bomb.)

The continuation of the Via Lambertesca and the Via Por Santa Maria is the Borgo Santi Apostoli. Medieval Florence, with its mysterious little alleyways all running off the parallel Via delle Terme, is very inviting. Going back down the Via delle Bombarde from the Via delle Terme leads to the square in front of ★ **Santi Apostoli** ❿; the Byzantine-style window slits above the side-aisle and the double window divided by a small pillar above the portal are immediately noticeable. An inscription on the left-hand side of the Romanesque stone facade announces that Charlemagne came here in 805, and founded the church.

Fortunately, the architectural alterations the church has received since that time have been harmonious. The three-aisled basilica with its marvellous open timber roof is divided by two sets of six Corinthian columns; the first pair were taken from the nearby Roman thermal springs, and the others are copies. A section of wall from the old Roman baths also forms part of the church's foundations. The left side-aisle has a large and harmoniously structured *tabernacle* by Andrea della Robbia's workshop (15th-century). The many impressive-looking tombstones set into the floor make it clear how important this ancient basilica is to Florence; the spark that makes the cart explode in the *Scoppio del Carro* festival on Easter Sunday is carried in a procession to the Duomo from this church.

The Borgo Santi Apostoli opens up into the Piazza Santa Trinità. Here, the Roman wall coming from the Via Porta Rossa makes a turn, and today's Via Tornabuoni, the most elegant street in Florence, still follows the route it took. This street looks exceptionally impressive at night, when the streetlights illuminate its facades. The piazza is dominated by the Column of Justice from the Baths of Caracalla in Rome, presented to Cosimo I by Pope Pius IV (the porphyry figure of *Justice* on the top is by Francesco Ferrucci, 1581). Three palazzi here represent three architectural phases of Florentine history.

The battlemented **Palazzo Spini-Feroni** ⓫ still has the air of a medieval fortress (late 13th-century). Opposite it, on the right-hand side of the Borgo Santi Apos-

35

Famous name in Via Tornabuoni

Palazzo Spini-Feroni

Seasonal vegetables
Door decoration at
Santa Trinità

From Ghirlandaio's Adoration

toli, the Palazzo Buondelmonti is the perfect example of a 15th-century Florentine patrician's house, with its separate ground floor, its Florentine windows with their distinctive 'eyebrows' and its loggia at the top. And on the next corner, at the junction of Via delle Terme and Via Porta Rossa, the **Palazzo Bartolini-Salimbeni** ⑫ is a clear example of the change of style that resulted from the Roman Renaissance in the 16th century: the decoration has become three-dimensional, resulting in a fascinating interplay of light and shadow across the reliefs on the facade (presently being renovated).

On the other side of the piazza is the baroque facade (by Buontalenti, 1593) of the church of ★ **Santa Trinità** ⑬. It is hard to believe that this church dates back to the 11th century. Last century, the interior facade of an earlier Romanesque structure was discovered on the site. The three-aisled building has a transept and a raised choir; the windows are Gothic, but the side-aisles and the choir have rectangular chapels – an architectural feature typical of the mendicant orders. Santa Trinità belonged to the Vallombrosan Order, which fought growing secularisation, and like the two other mendicant orders' churches it, too, lay outside the city walls. The church grew in importance because of its interior decoration: the orders invited rich patricians to decorate the chapels and thus salve their guilty consciences by serving God as well as humanity. The numerous works of art in the 17 chapels include:

Third chapel on the right (Cappella di San Luca): altarpiece of the *Madonna Enthroned with Four Saints* by Neri di Bicci (1466).

Fourth chapel on the right (Cappella della SS Annunziata): an *Annunciation* by Lorenzo Monaco (1422).

Second chapel to the right of the main altar (Sassetti Chapel): frescoes of the *Life of St Francis* by Domenico Ghirlandaio (1483); in the lunette above the altar, *St Francis Receiving the Rule of the Order from Pope Honorius III*. Ghirlandaio chose Florence as his backdrop here: the Loggia dei Lanzi and the Palazzo Vecchio can be made out, the Uffizi did not yet exist. The bald man on the right at the front is the merchant Sassetti, who commissioned the work, standing between his son and Medici prince Lorenzo the Magnificent. On the stairs is the poet Angelo Poliziano (Politian), the author of *Orfeo* (1475).

Sacristy (door on the left of the side exit): marble tomb of Onofrio Strozzi, by Lamberti (1421).

Second chapel to the left of the main altar (Scali Chapel): marble tomb of Benozzo Federighi, Bishop of Fiesole, by Luca della Robbia (1454–8), surrounded by enamelled terracotta mosaic on a gold ground.

Fifth chapel to the left (Cappella dell'Assunta): *Mary Magdalen*, a wooden statue by Desiderio da Settignano, completed by Benedetto da Maiano (late 15th-century).

Third chapel to the left (Davanzati Chapel): an *Annunciation* by Neri di Bicci (mid-15th-century); the tomb of Giuliano Davanzati (1444) was adapted from a 3rd-century Palaeochristian sarcophagus (Mithras cult) with a relief of the Good Shepherd.

Crypt (entrance in the nave): remains of the Romanesque church.

The Via del Parione passes to the right of the church. The former monastery cloister of Santa Trinità is now a study centre for young people. The Via Parioncino leads off to the right and into the Via del Purgatorio, which in turn leads to the ★★ **Palazzo Rucellai ⓮**, the former home of the Rucellai family of patricians, whose name is immortalised in the facade of Santa Maria Novella. Work began on this building in 1446, and architect Leon Battista Alberti (1404–72), with his detailed knowledge of Antiquity, lent a new dimension to Florentine secular architecture by giving the palazzo a Roman facade. The building has rusticated masonry, pilasters imitating classical orders, and graceful double windows on its upper storeys. The transition here from medieval palace-fortress to city palazzo is complete. Alberti also designed the Loggia dei Rucellai opposite, with its three arches.

37

To the left of the palazzo the Via dei Palchetti and the Via dei Federighi lead on to the Via della Spada, and on the corner is the **Cappella Rucellai ⓯**, also by Alberti (completed 1467). He designed the barrel vault and added the antique decor. The former church of San Pancrazio, which adjoins the square, is now a museum devoted to the work of sculptor and painter Marino Marini (1901–80). The Via della Spada leads back to the Via dei Tornabuoni, with its elegant shops. The latter then leads off to the left, to the Piazza Antinori. Dominating the right-hand side of the street here is the facade of **San Gaetano ⓰**, which was built between 1604 and 1648. In many ways it is another version of Santa Trinità; the rhythmic decoration, double pilasters and the generously-proportioned steps make the facade a great deal more monumental, though. The interior, in *pietra serena*, is surprisingly sombre. Directly opposite is the Early Renaissance **Palazzo Antinori ⓱**. The Antinori family have owned it since 1506, and still sell their wine here today.

San Gaetano facade

The Via Rondinelli now curves around gently to join the Via dei Cerretani; on the first street to the right is the church of **Santa Maria Maggiore ⓲**, a good church on which to practise recognising various different styles. The facade is Romanesque, the portal is 14th-century Gothic; the interior is a combination of baroque exuberance, Renaissance windows and Gothic pointed arches.

Route 3

★★★ Duomo – Via del Procònsolo – ★★ Bargello – Mercato Nuovo – ★ Palazzo Davanzati – ★★ Palazzo Strozzi – ★★ Orsanmichele – Casa Alighieri – Via del Corso – ★★★ Duomo

The **Via del Procònsolo** leaves the cathedral square at its southeast corner. On the left before the first intersection, the **Palazzo Nonfinito** ⑲ comes into view. Begun by Buontalenti in 1593, it was continued by Caccini according to designs by Scamozzi, but it remained uncompleted *(nonfinito)*. The gables above the ground-floor windows are a unique feature. Today this palazzo houses the Museo Nazionale di Antropologia ed Etnologia.

The Badia and the Bargello

On the opposite corner is a building often attributed to Brunelleschi, the ★ **Palazzo Pazzi** ⑳ ; in fact it was built by Giuliano da Maiano between 1462 and 1472 for Jacopo de' Pazzi. The latter took part in the notorious Pazzi conspiracy against the Medici in 1478 *(see page 11)* and was put to death. The facade is very elegant, with rectangular windows on the rusticated ground floor, graceful Rucellai double windows on the first floor, and round Renaissance windows on the second storey. The ★ **inner courtyard** is exceptionally handsome.

A short distance further along the Via del Procònsolo, two buildings that played important roles in the history of Florence stand opposite one another: the **Badia Fiorentina** ㉑ and the **Bargello** ㉒. The Badia, the oldest Benedictine monastery in Florence, was a centre of religious and spiritual power, while the Bargello (1255) became the centre of political and secular authority as a result of the political changes of 1250 *(see page 11)*. Very little remains of the original structure of the ★ **Badia** ㉑ apart from its outer walls. The building was radically altered in 1627. There is a good view of the ★ **campanile** from the cloister outside the main entrance: the storeys of this hexagonal tower clearly reveal the transition from Romanesque (early 14th-century) to Gothic. Because of the works of art it contains, the interior is almost a Renaissance museum: on the left of the entrance is *Madonna Appearing to St Bernard*, by Filippino Lippi (c 1486); on the right is the tomb of Pandolfini, from the workshop of Rossellino (1456); also a *Madonna and Saints* and the tombs of Bernardo Giugni and Conte Ugo, by Mino da Fiesole (1469). On the right of the main altar a door leads to the charming, two-storeyed ★ **Renaissance cloister**.

Madonna Appearing to St Bernard by Filippino Lippi

The Bargello

The massive, battlemented medieval fortress opposite is the famous ★★ **Bargello** ㉒ (Tuesday–Saturday 9am–2pm, Sunday and public holidays 9am–1pm), the oldest seat of government in the city, and today a national museum. The side facing the street and the tower were built by monk-architects Sisto and Ristoro from Santa Maria Novella (construction work began in 1255), and the rear section was added by Neri di Fioravanti (1332–45). Later, the interior was radically altered (mostly as a result of the building being converted into a prison, 16th–18th century). Since 1865 the Bargello has been a sculpture museum, and since 1986 one under scaffolding.

Just as awe-inspiring as many of the exhibits here is the medieval ★ **inner courtyard**, with its groin-vaulted arcades and its 14th-century stone staircase, with the coats-of-arms of the powerful along its walls.

The inner courtyard

Ground Floor: Sixteenth-century sculpture by Michelangelo and his Florentine contemporaries: Sansovino, Cellini, Giambologna, Bernini, Ammannati, etc.

First Floor: ecclesiastical works of art in ivory; palace chapel with ★ **high lectern**, decorated with intarsia. Donatello Hall (also containing Brunelleschi's entries for the Baptistry doors competition). Animals and *putti* by Giambologna in the loggia above the courtyard. Antique glassware in the room preceding the ceramics hall, which contains some astonishingly fine exhibits.

Displays in the Ceramics Hall

39

Second Floor: colourful enamelled terracottas of the Della Robbia school; Verrocchio room; small Renaissance bronzes; medal collection; seals, etc.

The Via del Procònsolo opens out into the Piazza San Firenze, which is dominated by two major edifices: on the left, **San Firenze 23**, a huge baroque building, built originally as an oratory for the Florentine Filippo Neri, who was canonised in 1622. Construction work began in the 17th century, and the facade dates from 1772–5. Today the building houses the law courts. Directly opposite is the ★ **Palazzo Gondi 24**, built by Giuliano da Sangallo (1490–1501). The massive rustication here and the huge, mys-

Bargello window

Souvenirs at the Mercato Nuovo

Fontana del Porcellino

Palazzo Davanzati exhibit

terious portals contrast typically with the subtly structured upper storeys – this palazzo is a fine example of the Florentine Renaissance style.

The route along the Via del Procònsolo as far as the Piazza San Firenze follows the course of the city's first Roman wall, which originally continued along the Via della Condotta all the way to the Piazza Santa Trinità. The Via della Condotta leads into the heart of medieval Florence, past the Via dei Cerchi with its small, elegant shops, and then across the Via dei Calzaiuoli. The street-name now changes to Via Porta Rossa, which leads on to the **Mercato Nuovo** ㉕, where lace, straw-work, leather goods and souvenirs can be bought. At the southeast corner where the Via Calimaruzza branches off towards the Piazza Signoria, the remains of a Roman city-gate (1st-century AD) can be seen in the basement of house No 3 (ask the doorman). The loggia, built on a square groundplan, was constructed between 1547 and 1551 for the sale of silk and gold, and is still used as a market booth today. The bronze boar is famous (the fountain is known familiarly as *Fontana del Porcellino*), and touching its snout is supposed to bring good luck. It is a copy of an original by Pietro Tacca (c 1612) which can be admired in the Uffizi. The boar's snout points in the direction of the **Palazzo dei Capitani di Parte Guelfa** ㉖, built as the official residence of the Captains of the Guelf Party in the 14th century (*see page 11*). The section with the Gothic windows is the oldest, and the rear part of the building on the corner of the Via delle Terme, based on a design by Brunelleschi, was added in the 15th century. The staircase and loggia on the other side of the building, facing the Via Carpaccio, are by Vasari (c 1589).

Further along the Via Porta Rossa is the ★**Palazzo Davanzati** ㉗, which since 1956 has been the Museo dell' Antica Casa Fiorentina (opening hours Tuesday–Saturday 9am–2pm, Sunday and public holidays 9am–1pm). It is the best surviving example of a 14th-century medieval nobleman's house in Florence. The house is built around a central courtyard, which could be cut off from the street in times of trouble; it contains the main stairway leading to the landings above. The well in the basement served all five floors of the house: a bucket was drawn up a hidden shaft. The kitchen was under the roof (the warmest place in the house), and various utensils are on display there. The first floor contains a whole series of 14th-century household items; much of the flooring is original.

Opposite the Palazzo Davanzati on the other side of the small square is the ★★ **Palazzo Strozzino** ㉘. Begun by Medici architect Michelozzo in 1458, the building was continued by Giuliano da Maiano (1462–5), and bears a clear resemblance to the Palazzo Medici-Riccardi.

On the corner, the Via degli Anselmi leads to the ★★ **Palazzo Strozzi** ㉙, built for wealthy patrician Filippo Strozzi (died 1491) and currently under scaffolding. Strozzi led the last attempt by the Republican exiles to abolish the Medici principate, and was defeated at the battle of Montemurlo. Construction work on the building began in 1489.

Palazzo Strozzi

The facade – a mixture of the rather unfriendly, tiny peepholes in the ground floor of the Palazzo Rucellai and the elegant upper floors of the Palazzo Medici-Riccardi – is by Giuliano Sangallo, and is crowned by a magnificent projecting cornice. The wrought-iron torch-holders were designed by Benedetto da Maiano.

The Via dei Strozzi opens out into the Piazza della Repubblica, created after the market quarter and the ghetto were demolished in the last century. The main post office is in the arcade on the right, and on Thursdays there is a flower and plant market here. On the other side of the square, the Via Orsanmichele branches off the Via Calimala to the left, and leads to the **Palazzo dell'Arte della Lana** ㉚, originally the headquarters of the wool merchants' guild, one of the city's wealthiest, with 30,000 employees and the *Agnus Dei* as its *stemma* (heraldic device). The building dates from 1308 and today is the headquarters of the Dante Society.

Next door to the palazzo is the tall rectangular church of ★★ **Orsanmichele** ㉛, originally built in 1337 as an open loggia for the sale of grain, and converted into a church in 1367. It was built on the site of the 9th-century San Michele ad hortum, and the arcades were enclosed by huge three-light Gothic ★ **tracery** windows in 1380. The various guilds were allowed to decorate the canopied niches outside the building, and the statues of patron saints they commissioned are a testimony to the skills of Florentine sculptors over a period of some 200 years.

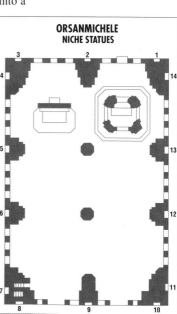

ORSANMICHELE
NICHE STATUES

★★ *Niche statues*

1 Ghiberti, *St John the Baptist* (1414–16)
2 *Tabernacle* by Donatello and Michelozzo (1425), *Doubting Thomas* by Verrocchio (c1480)
3 *St Luke* by Giambologna (1562)
4 *St Peter* by Donatello (1413)
5 *St Philip* by Nanni di Banco (1412)
6 *Four Crowned Saints* by Nanni di Banco (1408)
7 *St George* by Donatello (1416)
8 *St Matthew* by Ghiberti (1422)
9 *St Stephen* by Ghiberti (1426)
10 *St Elijah* by Nanni di Banco (c 1415)

Donatello's St Mark

11 *St Mark* by Donatello (1411–13)
12 *St James* by Piero Lamberti (c 1422)
13 *Madonna of the Rose* (1399, sculptor unknown)
14 *St John the Evangelist* by Baccio da Montelupo (1515)

The exterior of the building is decorated with 15th-century enamelled terracotta medallions, bearing the heraldic devices *(stemme)* of the various Florentine guilds, by Luca della Robbia (1399–1482) and his workshop. The interior (daily 8am–12 noon and 3–6.30pm) contains the impressive Gothic ★ **tabernacle** by Andrea Orcagna (1355–9), ornamented with marble and coloured glass. The reliefs show *Scenes from the Life of the Virgin*, and the altarpiece has been attributed to Bernardo Daddi. The two-aisled interior also contains an altar statue of the *Madonna and Child with St Anne* by Francesco da Sangallo (c 1526).

Daddi altarpiece, Orsanmichele

The Via dei Tavolini crosses the Via dei Cerchi and after the Piazza de' Cimatori turns into the Via Dante Alighieri; at the intersection with the Via Santa Margherita stands the **Torre della Castagna**, an ancient 13th-century tower, where the *priori* used to reside in 1382 before they moved to the Palazzo Vecchio. Opposite is the **Casa Alighieri ㉜**, reputedly the home of Dante's parents; the poet Dante Alighieri (1265–1321) probably grew up here. The building is now a museum (due to open in 1995 or 1996 after a year's closure; visitors are advised to check with the tourist office). The exhibits document the life of the poet, who was also an enthusiastic politician. In 1295 he joined the *Arte dei Medici e degli Speziali* (doctors' and apothecaries' guild), and in 1300 he was elected as one of the *priori* for two months. He was also a 'White Guelf', rejecting the German emperor but also not wanting to be subjugated by the pope. When the 'Black Guelfs' *(neri)* came to power in 1302 Dante was condemned to death, and went into exile. During the rest of his life he lived in Ravenna – where his grave lies – and also Bologna, Lucca, Verona and Venice.

Bust of Dante at Casa Alighieri

Directly opposite the house is the small church of **Santa Margherita de' Cerchi ㉝**, Dante's local church, where he probably got married. The Via Santa Margherita leads through an archway to the **Via del Corso**; on the left here is the church of **Madonna de' Ricci ㉞**, also known as Santa Margherita de' Ricci, with a porticoed facade dating from 1611. The interior was altered in the 18th century and is a fine example of neoclassicism, with painted ceiling, side altars, pillars and wrought-iron balustrades by Zanobi del Rosso (1769).

The Via del Corso extends as far as the Via de' Calzaiuoli, which then goes round to the right and leads back to the starting-point, the Piazza del Duomo.

Route 4

★★ Ponte Vecchio – Borgo San Jacopo – Ponte Santa Trinità – San Frediano – ★★★ Brancacci Chapel (Santa Maria del Carmine) – ★★ Santo Spirito – ★★ Palazzo Pitti – Fortezza di Belvedere – Santa Felicità – ★★ Ponte Vecchio

Just as Rome was built on a shallow ford of the River Tiber, the narrowest part of the Arno, where the ★★ **Ponte Vecchio** (the Old Bridge) now stands, formed part of an important trading route to Volterra as far back as Etruscan times. In Roman times the *Via Cassia* – the road connecting Rome with Florence – crossed the Arno here, and from the Early Middle Ages onwards there were several reports about the bridge being unable to withstand the Arno's floods. After the inundation of 1333, redevelopment work was decided on: to stem the floods, tall walls were built, as was the stone bridge still in existence today (built either by Neri di Fioravanti or Taddeo Gaddi). The other bank of the Arno, the so-called *Oltrarno*, had been settled long beforehand and was enclosed by the third

The Ponte Vecchio

43

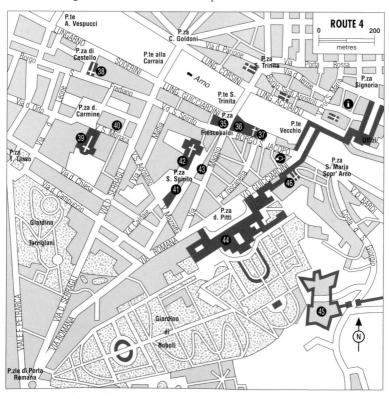

Peace on the Ponte Vecchio

Bust of Cellini

city wall, and so renting out the shops on the bridge was a useful source of extra income for the city-state. The shops were then sold off in around 1600, and this resulted in the adventurous-looking structures for which the Ponte Vecchio is famous today. In 1565 Vasari built the Corridoio for Cosimo I, the connecting section between the Uffizi and the Palazzo Pitti (*see page 31*) which crosses the Arno here. In 1593 the decision was taken to allow only goldsmiths, silversmiths and jewellers to use the shops on the Ponte Vecchio, which until then had been traditionally used by butchers. There is a monument in the middle of the bridge to one of the city's greatest goldsmiths, Benvenuto Cellini, whose *Perseus* can be admired in the Loggia dei Lanzi.

The **Borgo San Jacopo** runs parallel to the Arno through the quarter of the same name. Its narrow streets and ancient doors, with their charming terracottas (No 17 has a good *Annunciation*), lend historic atmosphere. The formerly Romanesque church of **San Jacopo sopr'Arno** ㉟ has a 13th-century portico; according to Vasari, its dome was a practice-run for Brunelleschi before he went on to do the big one on the cathedral.

At the end of the Borgo San Jacopo on the right, in front of the **Ponte di Santa Trinità**, is the Piazza Frescobaldi. A striking feature of the facade of the **Palazzo Frescobaldi** ㊱ is the imaginative design of the windows in the centre portal. The building, which dates back to the 13th century, was later given baroque additions.

At No 1 Lungarno Guicciardini is the **Palazzo Caponi** ㊲; the salon on the first floor was completely covered with allegorical frescoes in honour of the Capponi family by Bernardo Poccetti (1585). The Palazzo Lanfredini at No 9 still bears traces of Baccio d'Agnolo's bright graffiti decoration on its 16th-century facade.

Ponte Santa Trinità and Palazzo Corsini

After the Ponte alla Carraia the view across the Arno stretches as far as the green expanse of the Cascine public park. With its main entrance facing the Arno is **San Frediano in Cestello** 38, a bizarre-looking architectural complex consisting of an unfinished facade, a fine dome surmounted by a lantern and also a playful, disproportionately slender campanile. The building (1680–98) is Florentine baroque. The chapels inside are also domed, and were painted by 18th-century masters, as was the huge cupola above the crossing. The polychromatic marble altar has portals left and right extending up to the side walls. The west end has a fine organ-loft, and the third chapel on the left contains a 13th-century painted wooden statue of the *Smiling Madonna*.

On the right-hand side of the church, the Via di Cestello joins the Borgo San Frediano; follow the latter round to the left, and the first turn-off to the right leads into the piazza containing the church of **Santa Maria del Carmine** 39. This building, with its interesting rough stone facade, contains one of the greatest treasures of Italian painting in its transept, which together with the sacristy survived a fire unscathed in the year 1771. The ★★★ **Brancacci Chapel** (opening hours weekdays except Tuesday 10am–5pm, Sunday and public holidays 1–5pm; the popularity of the frescoes means that visitors are allowed only 15 minutes to see them; entrance to the right of the church portal), is easily on a par with Michelangelo's Sistine Chapel in Rome and Giotto's frescoes in the Cappella degli Scrovegni in Padua. The Brancacci, a family of wealthy silk merchants, commissioned painters Masolino da Panicale and Masaccio; the former had a style that was still traditionally Gothic, while Masaccio (1401–28) continued Giotto's early realism via the perfect application of the new rules of perspective, and he thus forms the artistic link between Giotto and Michelangelo. His frescoes gain their particularly vivid, animated quality from the clever use of light and shade *(chiaroscuro)* to create depth.

Tribute Money by Masaccio

The content of the frescoes *(see overleaf)* is closely associated with the family who commissioned them. The newly wealthy class of merchants to whom the Brancacci belonged had theological problems, because the church was opposed to the idea of anyone earning interest – even though that was the mainstay of the city's prosperity. Bearing this in mind, Masaccio's *Tribute Money* fresco and also *St Peter Distributing Alms* almost seem to justify the practice; after all, Christ himself acknowledged the necessity of paying tribute money, and the Brancacci family were distributing their worldly goods too,

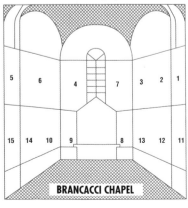

BRANCACCI CHAPEL

The Raising of Tabitha

St Peter Enthroned

by commissioning this magnificent chapel for all believers. Work on the frescoes was broken off abruptly in 1427 for reasons that are unknown; the cycle was only completed some 50 years later, after Masaccio's death, by Filippino Lippi (1483). *See plan on previous page.*

Frescoes by Masolino

1 *Temptation of Adam and Eve*
2 (with Masaccio) *The Raising of Tabitha*
3 (with Masaccio) *The Healing of the Cripple*
4 *The Sermon of St Peter*

Frescoes by Masaccio

5 *The Expulsion from Paradise*
6 *The Tribute Money*
7 *The Baptism of the Neophytes*
8 *St Peter Distributing Alms*
9 *St Peter Healing the Sick with his Shadow*
10 *St Peter Enthroned* (the friar with the red hood to the left of the saint is thought to be Masaccio himself)

Frescoes by Filippino Lippi

11 *Release of St Peter from Prison*
12 *St Peter Arguing with Simon* (self-portrait of Lippi to the right of the painting)
13 *Crucifixion of St Peter*
14 *Resurrection of the Son of Theophilus*
15 *St Peter in Prison Visited by St Paul*

The Cappella Corsini in the left transept of the church by Pier Francesco Silvani (1675–83) contains a dome fresco by Luca Giordano, *Apotheosis of St Andrew Corsini of Fiesole*; the three large marble reliefs with *Scenes From the Life of St Andrew* are by Giovanni Battista Foggini (1652–1725).

The sacristy, also saved from the flames in 1771, is definitely worth a visit: the altarpiece to the right of the entrance, *Madonna Enthroned with Saints*, has been attributed to Andrea da Firenze, master of the Spanish Chapel. The frescoes in the room date from the time of its construction (13th to 14th-century); works in the adjacent rooms include frescoes by Filippino Lippi and his workshop. On the right-hand side of the presbytery is the monumental tomb (by Benedetto da Rovezzano, 16th-century) of Piero Soderini, the last *Gonfaloniere* of the Republic, who died and was buried in exile in 1522.

From the church square the Via Santa Monica leads to the Via de' Serragli, passing the tiny church of **Santa Monaca** ⓴ with its charming Renaissance facade. After the intersection the street becomes the Via San Agostino, and opens out into the elegant Piazza Santo Spirito, a fine leafy square to relax in; there's also a vegetable market here in the mornings. Towering above the square to the right is the **Palazzo Guadagni** ⓵ , a model 16th-century Florentine mansion, probably built by Cronaca (1503). It has fine graffiti decoration on its facade (hidden by scaffolding at the time of writing) and also a fine top-floor loggia beneath its projecting roof.

Palazzo Guadagni

The rather modest 18th-century facade of ★★ **Santo Spirito** ⓶ can be seen at the top of the piazza. The previous building on this site was destroyed by fire in the 13th century, and Brunelleschi was then commissioned to design a new church in 1444 for the Augustinians. He died two years later, however, and in 1487 his design was finally realised – not all that successfully – by Antonio Manetti, Giovanni da Gaiole and Salvi d'Andrea. Salvi d'Andrea built the dome as he thought fit and missed out the facade entirely; the slender campanile is a contribution by Baccio D'Agnolo (1503–17). Brunelleschi wanted to build a counterpart to San Lorenzo, which would face it from the opposite bank of the Arno. It was not to be. After his death the whole edifice was pointed in a different direction, and neither of the two churches has ever had its facade completed.

Santo Spirito

The interior of Santo Spirito reveals Brunelleschi's sure command of form; the convincing clarity of San Lorenzo is surpassed here by the feeling of order and harmony, the austere use of colour, and the perspective of the colonnades and vaulted aisles. The master architect replaced the walls here with a continuous series of 40 chapels around the entire church (with the exception of the portal), anticipating the baroque style in his search for the mastery of space. Some

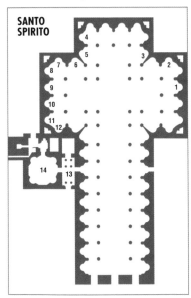

SANTO SPIRITO

Interior of the dome

say that Brunelleschi, with his famous centralised structures, was not all that fond of this three-aisled church in the shape of a Latin cross; the groundplan clearly shows, however, that Santo Spirito was designed as a centralised building with a transept attached, like St Peter's in Rome, and the original Greek cross shape with transepts of equal length was then altered during actual construction, when one transept was lengthened. This also explains why the interior facade and the rear wall of the choir jar with each other: the choir wall was only designed to harmonise with the transepts.

The many paintings inside this church provide a glimpse into the work of several of the less well-known masters of the Renaissance; the gradual transition in the backgrounds from smooth gold to perspective landscape appears here in many variations.

Selection *(see plan on previous page)*

1. *Madonna and Child with the Young St John, Saints, and the Donors* by Filippino Lippi (1490)
2. Marble sarcophagus of Neri Capponi by Bernardo Rossellino (1457)
3. *Madonna and Saints* by Lorenzo di Credi (early 16th-century)
4. *Annunciation*, Florentine school (15th-century)
5. *Nativity*, Domenico Ghirlandaio school (15th-century)
6. *Madonna with Child, Angels and Saints,* attributed to Francesco Granacci (late 15th-century)
7. *St Monica Founding the Order of Augustinian Nuns* by Francesco Botticini (15th-century)
8. *Madonna with Child and Saints* by Cosimo Rosselli (15th-century)
9. Marble altar by Andrea Sansovino (1492) in the shape of a triumphal arch
10. *Trinity* attributed to Raffaellino del Garbo (1470–1525)
11. *Madonna with Angels, St Bartholomew, St Nicholas of Bari and Two Donors* by Raffaellino del Garbo
12. *Madonna with Child and Four Saints* by Raffaellino del Garbo
13. Vestibule by Andrea Sansovino
14. Sacristy by Giuliano da Sangallo and Cronaca (1489): domed octagon and double pilasters in Florentine Renaissance style

To the left of the church is the entrance to the ★ **Cenacolo di Santo Spirito** (Tuesday–Saturday 9am–2pm, Sunday and public holidays 8am–1pm) the former refectory, now a museum. On the wall at the back is a magnificent

Crucifixion fresco, and also a *Last Supper*, both attributed to Andrea Orcagna (c 1360). The sculptures on display here are rare architectural and decorative fragments from the Romanesque and pre-Romanesque periods.

Next to the facade the Via de' Michelozzi branches off to intersect with the Via Maggio; the latter's real name is actually the Via Maggiore (Big Street), because of its sharp contrast with the tiny medieval alleys around it. It used to be the main traffic artery leading to the city centre on the other side of the Arno, and was used for processions, tournaments and games. A stroll along here today is definitely worthwhile if only to admire the many elegant antique shops, and the facade of house No 26, the **Casa Bianca Cappello** ㊸, should certainly not be missed either; it was designed by Buontalenti (c 1570), and was once the home of famous courtesan Bianca Cappello, the mistress of Francesco I, Duke of Florence (1541–87). The graffiti decoration is by Poccetti (1548–1612).

Palazzo Pitti

After its intersection with the Via Maggio the Via de' Michelozzi becomes the Sdrucciolo de' Pitti, a quiet little street at the end of which the immense ★★ **Palazzo Pitti** ㊹, (Tuesday–Friday 9am–2pm, Sunday and public holidays 9am–1pm) with its 205-m (670-ft) wide facade, suddenly comes into view. The Pitti were rivals of the Medici, and commissioned Brunelleschi to design the main section of the palace around the year 1440: seven bays, with three doorways and four windows on the ground floor, and seven windows on the upper ones. This was in keeping with the architectural style of the time, even though Brunelleschi had been told to outdo all the other palazzi in Florence. The Medici responded with the ten-bay Palazzo Medici-Riccardi (*see page 53*). The Pitti family's fortunes then waned, and they were forced to stop building in 1470, finally even having to sell the palazzo in 1549 to Elenora of Toledo, wife of Cosimo I. The building was immediately extended, with a feeling for style that was rare for that time: the same materials and forms used in the central section designed by Brunelleschi were simply enlarged. This was done by Ammannati in 1560, by Giulio and Alfonso Parigi in the 17th century, and by Giuseppe Ruggieri in the 18th; the building thus received its present-day appearance. It looks far more forbidding than the palazzi of the Medici, Rucellai and Strozzo in the city centre, for two main reasons: first, it is built on a rise, which makes it far more monumental, and second, the upper floors lack the usual double windows and finer structuring, and thus do not form much of a contrast to the forbidding-looking rustication at ground level.

The Palazzo Pitti today contains museums with first-class exhibits, and is itself a museum, documenting as it does four centuries of magnificent interior design. The en-

Empire chair, Galleria Palantina

Raphael's Maddalena Doni

trance is on the right-hand side of the inner courtyard; a grand staircase leads up to the museum floors.

The **★★ Galleria Palatina** *(Galleria Pitti)* takes up the entire left-hand side of the palace. Before being converted into galleries, these rooms were magnificent palace apartments, and so a visit is worthwhile for the interior decoration alone, which was executed in the high baroque style by Pietro da Cortona (1596–1669). It served as a model for many European palaces. The art gallery, with its works by many of the world's most famous painters, adds an extra aesthetic dimension to the place, though for many it can seem too much of a good thing: the paintings have been hung simply with an eye to decoration, with no connection in content or otherwise, nor any relation to the rooms or the decoration around them. Unfortunately the artistic effect of several of the masterpieces on display here gets lost quite often, and art-lovers are best advised to concentrate on their own favourites and to try to ignore the over-decorative surroundings as best they can.

The Galleria Palatina contains masterpieces by Titian, Giorgione, Raphael, Rubens, Van Dyck, Rosso Fiorentino, Murillo, Fra Bartolomeo, Andrea del Sarto, Velázquez, Caravaggio, Allori, Filippino Lippi, Luca Signorelli, Guido Reni, Paolo Veronese and Antonio Canova.

On the right-hand side of the floor are the Appartamenti ex Reali, or Former Royal Apartments. Four centuries of royal life can be observed here: in the 16th century the Medici moved into the 15th-century Early Renaissance building and decorated it in accordance with contemporary taste; later on, in the 18th century, the Austrian grand dukes resided here until Italian unification in 1860; and the last potentates to live here were the kings of Italy up until World War I. The interior decoration in the *appartamenti* here reflects the tastes of each epoch.

On the second floor, more modern paintings are on display in the **Galleria d'Arte Moderna** (Gallery of Modern Art), but since this gallery was founded in 1860, 'modern' actually means late 18th- and 19th-century works (sculptures, paintings, arts and crafts).

A series of rooms on the ground floor of the Palazzo Pitti were lavishly decorated on the occasion of the grand marriage of Ferdinando II in 1634, and today they form the **Museo degli Argenti** (Silver Museum). The 17th-century frescoes here glorify the Medici family. The exhibits include priceless works of art made with precious stones, ivory and metals from the treasury of Ferdinando III and of the prince-bishops of Salzburg.

On the hillside behind the Palazzo Pitti lie the magnificent **★★ Boboli Gardens** (Giardino di Boboli) (June–August 9am–7.30pm; April, May, September 9am–6.30pm; March, October 9am–5.30pm; November to

February 9am–4.30pm) laid out on the order of Elenora of Toledo by Ammannati, then by Buontalenti and Alfonso Parigi. The biggest public park in the centre of Florence, these gardens are among the finest in Italy.

It is best to enter from the north wing of the palace, where the path follows the final stretch of the corridor from the Pitti to the Palazzo Vecchio. Beneath its walls is the so-called Fontana del Bacco (Bacchus Fountain), actually a statue of the pot-bellied court dwarf of Cosimo I, and a little further on is the Grotta del Buontalenti, an imaginative and artistic grotto created in the Mannerist style by Buontalenti (1583–8), with casts of Michelangelo's *Slaves*, frescoes by Poccetti and statues by Bandinelli. *Paris and Helen* (by Vincenzo de' Rossi, 1560) face one another in the second cave, while *Venus* (by Giambologna, 1573) can be seen emerging from her bath in the third one.

The path now winds its way uphill, passing the Anfiteatro (Amphitheatre) laid out like a Roman circus and decorated with antique statues (or copies). The view gives an idea of just how majestic the setting once used to be for performances staged in the palace courtyard. The path leads on up to the Neptune Fountain; the bronze statue of the sea-god is by Stoldo Lorenzi (1565). At the top of the garden is a colossal statue of *Abundance* by Giambologna, completed by Pietro Tacca (1636).

The path left leads to the rococo *Kaffeehaus*, left here by the Austrians in 1776, with its terrace and stunning views of the centre of Florence. Above it loom the imposing walls of the **Fortezza di Belvedere** ㊺, which the Medici had built between 1590 and 1595, not to enjoy the magnificent panorama it affords, but to fire on the city in the event of uprisings. This fortified villa was designed by Buontalenti, and today is used for exhibitions.

51

Statue of Abundance by Giambologna

Amphitheatre at the Boboli Gardens

Santa Felicità: Virgin by Pontormo

Santa Felicità door decoration

Barrel vaulting in the nave

Leaving the Fortezza di Belvedere, keep to the left, staying within the ring of fortifications, and then stroll downhill along the Costa San Giorgio. This is a nice quiet part of the city (a rarity for Florence) with the odd fine view and picturesque corner. One eventually emerges at the ancient church of **Santa Felicità** ㊻, which stands on the site of an Early Christian cemetery. The church underwent alterations in the 11th and 14th centuries before it was given its present-day appearance in the 18th century by Ferdinando Ruggieri (1736). The Corridoio Vasariano (*see page 31*) goes past this church and thus had to be built into it; the Medici could participate in the services held here via the golden grille on the rear wall. Ruggieri built a single-aisled interior with a barrel vault, trapezoid windows and projecting balconies, with a repeated 'grille' motif – possibly in anticipation of neoclassicism.

In the Cappella Capponi (first chapel on the right), designed by Brunelleschi in 1425 in his favourite centralised manner, there is a fine Mannerist *Deposition* by Pontormo (1538), who also painted the *Annunciation* fresco in the dome; three of the Evangelists in the tondi of the cupola are also by him, and the fourth (with the angel) is by Agnolo Bronzino. The sacristy (off the right transept) contains a polyptych of the *Madonna and Child with Saints* by Taddeo Gaddi (14th-century), and also *St Felicity and her Seven Sons* by Neri di Bicci (15th-century).

On the parvis, which is only a few steps away from the Ponte Vecchio, some fragments of palaeochristian tomb inscriptions are on display (4th to 5th-century).

Route 5

*** Duomo – ** Palazzo Medici-Riccardi – ** San
Lorenzo – ** Santa Maria Novella – * Ognissanti –
Lungarno Corsini – ** Ponte Vecchio

Next to the Baptistry the Via de' Martelli leaves the Piazza del Duomo and heads north. At No 22r along this
busy street is the Libreria Marzocco, one of the best book-
shops in the city. At the first intersection, the ** **Palazzo**
Medici-Riccardi 47 (entrance in the inner courtyard;
weekdays except Wednesday 9am–1pm and 3–5pm, Sunday and public holidays 9am–12noon) comes into view.
This building was the seat of the Medici (their coat-of-
arms can still be seen halfway up the wall on the corner)
until they moved into the Palazzo Vecchio in 1540. Cosimo
the Elder asked Michelozzo to build the palazzo in 1444,
and he designed a square building in accordance with contemporary taste. The original sides were the length of the
facade with its 10 bays along the Via de' Gori; the Riccardi family later enlarged the building by adding a further seven bays along the Via Cavour (1684–9). The

Palazzo Medici-Riccardi

53

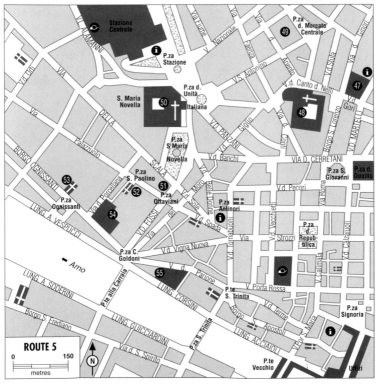

ROUTE 5

0 — 150

metres

Statue at the Palazzo Medici-Riccardi

Street market, Piazza San Lorenzo

A city of artisans

rustication on the ground floor is 8m (26ft) high, and has round arches set into it; the ones on the corners were open, and Michelangelo filled them with playful windows in 1517. The upper storeys have double-windows, and the rustication higher up is altogether more gentle. The cornice, modelled on Antiquity, completes the structure. Originally square in shape, it protected the inner courtyard with its rhythmic, round-arched arcades adorned with medallions. The Riccardi family's alterations left only one 15th-century jewel behind: Michelozzo's ★★ **Cappella** on the first floor.

The decorative frescoes (1459–60) showing the *Procession of the Magi to Bethlehem* are the masterpiece of Benozzo Gozzoli, and they depict many contemporary personalities including the Medici family – young Lorenzo the Magnificent on the white horse, his father Piero di Cosimo behind him wearing the red beret, and the latter's brother Giovanni. This seemingly endless triumphal procession across a Tuscan landscape is closely associated with political events of the time: all forces were then being mobilised to recapture Constantinople, capital of the former East Roman Empire, which had fallen to the Turks in 1453.

In the second courtyard – the one in the newer part of the building – the Galleria on the first floor is definitely worth a visit. Luca Giordano (1632–1705) glorified the second Medici dynasty in a superbly-executed series of frescoes on the barrel vault.

The tiny Via de' Gori leads along the battlemented garden wall of the Palazzo Medici to the Piazza San Lorenzo, filled with a busy street market selling clothing and souvenirs. The line of houses here follows the route taken by the second city wall. The seated statue (1540) of Giovanni delle Bande Nere is by Baccio Bandinelli; the most

distinctive feature here, though, is the archaic-looking, incomplete facade of ★★ **San Lorenzo** ⓭, consecrated by St Ambrose, Bishop of Milan, in the year 393.

The present structure was commissioned by the Medici from 1420 onwards, according to designs by Brunelleschi. After the latter's death his work was continued by Antonio Manetti (1447–69) and then by Michelangelo (c 1520–34), who rounded off the whole project by adding not just two sacristies but also the Medici Chapels and the Biblioteca Medicea-Laurenziana. In 1740 the campanile was added by Ferdinando Ruggieri.

It was inside San Lorenzo that Brunelleschi first presented the formal language he had derived from Florentine Romanesque (*see page 83*). To achieve a rational spatial clarity he used round arches, pillars, capitals, pilasters, entablature and round windows; the side walls correspond with the arcades of the nave.

San Lorenzo

The interior of the church

1　Interior facade designed by Michelangelo (c1518)
2　*Marriage of the Virgin* by Rosso Fiorentino (1494–1540); Gothic tomb-slab of the organist Francesco Landini (died 1397)
3　Tabernacle by Desiderio da Settignano, prototype in central perspective (1461)
4　Main altar in polychrome marble (1787); crucifix by Baccio da Montelupo (16th-century)
5　Memorial slab to Cosimo the Elder by Verrocchio; Donatello's sarcophagus below
6　*Madonna*, in polychrome wood (14th-century)
7　*Annunciation* by Filippo Lippi (1406–69)
8　*Martyrdom of St Lawrence* fresco by Bronzino (1503–72)
9/10　★★ **Pulpits** by Donatello (c 1460) and his workshop, with bronze relief of the Passion. Brunelleschi created the cube-shaped ★★ **Old Sacristy** with its hemispherical dome, and Donatello was responsible for the sculpture (medallions, altar, portals, statues)
11　Marble sarcophagus of the parents of Cosimo il Vecchio, by Cavalcanti (1433)
12　Sarcophagus of Giovanni and Piero de' Medici by Verrocchio (1469–72), made from porphyry, bronze, marble and green serpentine
13　Little chapel with lavabo by the Verrocchio school. The cloister then leads to the ★★ **Biblioteca Medicea-Laurenziana** (opening hours weekdays 10am–1pm)

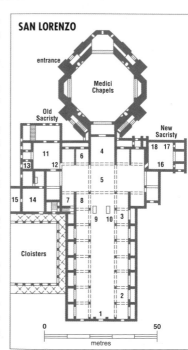

SAN LORENZO

entrance

Medici Chapels

Old Sacristy

New Sacristy

Cloisters

0　　　　　　50

metres

*Medici Chapels:
entrance and ceiling*

14 Library vestibule, with the surprising solution Michelangelo chose for the staircase (1524–6)

15 Reading Room: walls, floor, ceiling and inlaid desks all designed by Michelangelo (begun in 1524, consecrated in 1571)

The entrance to the ★★ **Cappelle Medicee** (Medici Chapels) is outside the church, in the Piazza della Madonna degli Aldobrandini (weekdays except Monday 9am–2pm, Sunday and public holidays 9am–1pm).

It was Grand Duke Cosimo I who first insisted on a further mausoleum for the Medici family, and the ★ **Cappella dei Principi** (Mausoleum of Medici grand dukes) was eventually designed by Don Giovanni di Medici, the illegitimate son of Cosimo I (1602), and then begun by Matteo Nigetti in 1604. Work continued until as late as 1836. This imposing-looking octagonal structure with its dome contains some incomparably fine pietra-dura work – the sheer opulence here outshines the gloom.

Sarcophagi to the left of the apse: Cosimo I (died 1574); Francesco (died 1587); Cosimo III (died 1723).

Sarcophagi to the right of the apse: Ferdinando I (died 1609); Cosimo II (died 1620); Ferdinando II (died 1670).

Attached to the north transept is the ★★ **New Sacristy**. This was Michelangelo's first architectural commission, and while he employed the same basic centralised structure of Brunelleschi's Old Sacristy, he also rendered it with sculptural additions that endow this family chapel with a magnificent grandeur. Double pilasters accentuate the idealised statues of the city's rulers.

16 Sarcophagus of Giuliano de' Medici with the allegorical figures *Day* and *Night*. *Night* is associated with Michelangelo's shock at the city's loss of its freedom in 1531

17 Sarcophagus of Lorenzo de' Medici, Duke of Urbino, with the reclining allegorical figures of *Dawn* and *Dusk*. Lorenzo appears as a Thinker

18 Architectural monument to Lorenzo the Magnificent and his brother Giuliano, who died during the Pazzi conspiracy in 1478. The work is incomplete; the *Madonna and Child* are by Michelangelo, while the statues of St Cosmas and St Damian are by Montorsoli and Raffaello da Montelupo (1533)

*Take your pick at the
Mercato Centrale*

The Via dell'Ariento, packed with market stalls like the rest of this area, branches off towards the **Mercato Centrale** ⑳, the central food market; to the left, the narrow Via Sant'Antonio leads off to the Piazza dell'Unità Italiana, where there is a view of the modern station of Santa Maria Novella.

★★ *Santa Maria Novella* 🗐

This is the most important Gothic church in Tuscany. A mendicant order basilica like Santa Croce (*see page 71*), it was built outside the city walls. The facade and the parvis can be reached by walking around the cemetery. There are two obelisks on the parvis: Cosimo I was fond of horse-racing and had them placed there as turning markers, serving the same purpose to those of the Circus Maximus in Rome (1608).

Exterior

Santa Maria Novella

Construction work on the present-day version of the church (a building on this site is first mentioned in the 10th century) began in 1246. The Dominicans, who were given the property, chose the simple and unadorned style favoured by mendicant orders – no grandeur, purely functional architecture, and simple rectangles instead of polygonal variety. The facade of Santa Maria Novella was begun in 1300, but remained unfinished – until the rich patrician Giovanni Rucellai secured a future place in paradise for himself by collecting together some earthly means to have it completed. He gave architect Leon Battista Alberti this commission in 1458 – on condition that he retained the already completed lower part of the facade and also the large round window. The tiny dichromatic Gothic niches with two narrow doors can be seen in the lowest section; Alberti accentuated this section by adding a powerful main portal with pillars. Its entablature, combined with the pillars on the outside of the facade, gives the ground floor an entirely new look. Alberti placed the round window at the centre of an eye-catching mezzanine with square patterns. He had studied San Miniato very closely: the connection between the lower floor and the gable there is solved by sloping diagonals. Alberti – possibly as a result of his knowledge of Antiquity – made a historic decision and chose scrolls instead. This means of solving the problem of connecting different levels on facades was imitated everywhere.

Interior

The raised section of the floor from the seventh bay onwards is a reminder that the friars' choir began there, before it fell victim to Vasari's 'modernisation' between 1565 and 1572, along with the rood screen. This church contains some very valuable works of art; the mendicant orders allowed wealthy families to use chapels – and those families spared no expense in decorating them. The Rucellai managed to have their family emblem (a billowing ship's sail) included alongside that of the Medici (a ring with ostrich feathers) in a magnificent inlaid frieze along the entire length of the facade.

Decoration inside Santa Maria Novella

Scenes from the Life of the Virgin by Ghirlandaio

The cloisters

Works of art (a selection): the *Nativity* above the portal on the inside has been attributed to Filippo Lippi (15th-century); the *Coronation of the Virgin* at the rose window is by Andrea da Firenze (c 1365); in the second side-altar on the right is the tomb of Beata Villana by Bernardo Rossellino and workshop (1451). Next to the fifth pillar on the right is the entrance to the Cappella della Pura (1474), which contains a 14th-century Madonna that supposedly has miraculous powers; access from here to the cemetery. Stairs in the right transept lead down to the Cappella Rucellai (14th-century), containing the bronze tomb-slab of Lionardo Dati by Ghiberti; the famous *Madonna Rucellai* by Duccio di Buoninsegnia (early 14th-century) used to hang above the altar here before it was moved to the Uffizi. The Cappella Strozzi (on the right of the main altar) contains frescoes executed by Filippo Lippi between 1497 and 1502: in the vault are *Adam, Noah, Abraham and Jacob*; on the right-hand wall is the *Martyrdom of St John the Evangelist*; and behind the altar is the elaborately carved tomb of Filippo Strozzi by Benedetto da Maiano (1491–3). At the main altar is a bronze crucifix by Giambologna (14th-century) and superb frescoes by Domenico Ghirlandaio (1485–90). In the Cappella Gondi, to the left of the main altar, is a wooden crucifix by Brunelleschi (his only sculpture to survive in wood, carved at some time between 1410 and 1425), traditionally thought to have been carved to show Donatello how the Redeemer should be represented. Brunelleschi is said to have called Donatello's crucifix in Santa Croce 'a mere peasant on the cross'.

A flight of steps in the left transept leads to the Cappella Strozzi di Mantova, containing frescoes of *The Last Judgement*, *Hell* and *Paradise* (based on Dante's *Divine Comedy*) by Nardo di Cione (1357); the chapel is, however, closed for restoration until at least 1996. In the sacristy (access via the left transept), the crucifix is an early work by Giotto (before 1300) and the lavabo in terracotta with landscape is by Giovanni della Robbia (1498). On the way back to the main portal, the pulpit can be admired (second to last pillar, on the left): it was designed by no less a person than Brunelleschi, in 1443, and the reliefs show *Scenes from the Life of the Virgin*. Behind the pillar, in the third side-altar from the end, there is an epoch-making fresco: Masaccio's ★★★ *Trinity*, which he painted just before his death (1428). Here, Brunelleschi's architectural aesthetic has been rendered in paint: this was the first time since Antiquity that a painter had ever used perspective.

On the left-hand side of the church facade is the entrance to the cloisters, which today are the ★ **Museo di Santa Maria Novella** (opening hours: weekdays except

Friday 9am–2pm, Sunday and public holidays 8am–1pm). The Chiostro Verde (Green Cloister), so named because of the predominant colour of the frescoes painted here by Paolo Uccello and his workshop (14th-century) on the theme of *Genesis*, was badly damaged in the floods of 1966. At least Uccello's *Diluvio Universale* was saved from destruction. What remained can be admired in the refectory, where Uccello's *Sacrifice of Noah* is also on display (turn left at the end of the cloister).

The entrance to the newly restored **Cappellone degli Spagnoli** (Spanish Chapel) is marked by sturdy Gothic columns similar to those in the Duomo and Orsanmichele.

Originally the Dominican friars' chapter-house, this chapel was built between 1348 and 1355, during the heyday of the Gothic period. Andrea da Firenze completed the paintings here in 1365; the historic year of 1348, when the population of Florence alone was reduced from 100,000 to just 45,000 by a plague outbreak, also plays a part in the frescoes here. The huge gap in art history after Giotto died in 1337 was a direct result of the plague, as was the yearning for security and order so clearly expressed in these frescoes.

59

The wall on the right shows the Church Militant and Triumphant (the Florence Cathedral depicted here was never built) and the glorification of the actions of the Dominicans; in the foreground behind a group of kneeling pilgrims are the presumed portraits of Cimabue, Giotto, Boccaccio, Dante and Petrarch; the flock of the faithful is watched over by the Dominican friars, symbolised by dogs attacking heretical wolves. *Domini Canes* means the Hounds of the Lord – an apt name for the friars who saw their role as defenders of the faith against heresy.

The opposite wall shows the *Triumph of Divine Wisdom* and the *Glorification of St Thomas Aquinas*; facing the entrance is the *Ascent to Calvary*, the *Crucifixion* and the *Descent into Limbo*; on the vault, the *Resurrection*. The frescoes in the Spanish Chapel are the most important work by the otherwise little-known artist Andrea da Firenze (died 1377, sometimes also called Andrea di Bonaiuto), who was influenced by the Sienese school of painting.

Andrea da Firenze: fresco in the Spanish Chapel

Opposite the church, on the piazza, is the **Loggia di San Paolo** ⑤, the former entrance to the Spedale San Paolo dei Convalescenti, a kind of parallel institution to Brunelleschi's Ospedale degli Innocenti.

The route now leads through an atmospheric part of Florence that is relatively free of tourists. Turn off the Via dei Fossi down the Via Palazzuolo with its piazza and church of **San Paolino** ⑤. This building, which looks rather odd from the outside, is even more surprising inside (its present form dates from the late 17th century); the unadorned interior with its apse, transept, dome and central

Ognissanti facade

Coronation of the Virgin

Admiring the interior

Palazzo Corsini

nave has a connecting balustrade running all the way round that almost seems to be holding everything together (1669–93). The first and second chapels on the right contain some rather grisly reminders of the transience of human existence.

The Via San Paolino passes the right-hand side of the church and then turns right into the Via della Porcellana; this part of the city contains many small workshops. After the street has emerged into the Borgo Ognissanti, the church of ★ **Ognissanti** 🟟 is just a few steps away. Its harmonious facade by Matteo Nigetti (1638) contains Renaissance and baroque elements; the *Coronation of the Virgin* above the portal is a product of the della Robbia school (c 1515). Inside, the second altar on the left contains the tomb of the Vespucci family, adorned by a *Madonna della Misericordia* fresco by Ghirlandaio. The boy whose head appears between the Madonna and the man in the dark cloak is supposed to be Amerigo Vespucci, the Medici agent in Seville who followed Columbus's routes, and after whom America was named. On the same side is Botticelli's *St Augustine* (1480) and opposite, another Ghirlandaio, this time of *St Hieronymus* (1480); Sandro Botticelli (died 1510) is buried in the family tomb (with the round slab) in the last chapel on the right.

The refectory in the cloister (entrance on the left of the facade) contains a ★ *Last Supper* by Ghirlandaio (1480) (Monday, Tuesday, Saturday 9am–noon). The delightful background includes Christian symbols of plants and birds.

Piazza Ognissanti contains a 20th-century version of Hercules fighting the Lion; the view from here across to the other bank and the massive San Frediano should not be missed. The Borgo Ognissanti is where Florence originally began to prosper, because from the 11th century onwards Benedictine monks ran cloth- and wool-manufacturing enterprises in this part of the city. Today, the many tasteful and elegant shops make a stroll back through this quarter a real pleasure; at No 26 there is a fine Italian Art Nouveau house, and No 20, the **Ospedale di San Giovanni di Dio** 🟤 , has a superb early 18th-century baroque staircase.

From the Piazza Goldoni (which contains a statue of the author dating from 1873) the route then continues along the bank of the river via the **Lungarno Corsini** as far as the huge **Palazzo Corsini** 🟟 , built in grandiose Roman baroque style (mid 17th-century). The facade is crowned by statues and has a terrace overlooking the river.

The route ends a little further along the Arno at the ★★**Ponte Vecchio**. From here the Via Por Santa Maria, Via Calimala and the Via Roma all lead directly back to the starting point at the ★ ★ ★ **Duomo**.

Route 6

★★★ Duomo – ★ Galleria dell'Accademia – San Marco – Giardino dei Semplici (Orto Botanico) – SS Annunziata – ★ Spedale degli Innocenti – ★ Museo Archeologico – ★ Santa Maria de'Pazzi – Sant' Ambrogio – Loggia del Pesce – ★★★ Duomo

The Via Ricasoli branches away north of the ★★★ **Duomo**, passing the Teatro Niccolini on the way, and just before the intersection with the Via degli Alfani the mighty **Palazzo Gerini** 56, with its nine-bay facade, appears. The portals on the ground floor flank seven windows with triangular gables, and the nine round windows on the first floor, reinforced with rustication, complete the facade (by Baccio d'Agnolo, 16th-century). The fact that the rustication has 'moved up' here, from the ground to the first floor, shows that it was used purely decoratively rather than for any functional purpose.

A tempting distraction

In the Via degli Alfani, next door to the Luigi Cherubini Conservatory, is the entrance to the museum **Opificio delle Pietre Dure** 57 (weekdays 9am–2pm; closed Sunday; presently closed for renovation), which is housed in a former monastery. Inlaid precious stones form the

61

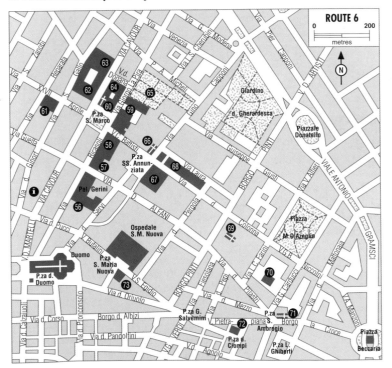

Casts in the Galleria dell'Accademia

David

Sculpture detail in the Galleria dell'Accademia

heart of this collection; pietra-dura was not only used for decorative designs and coats-of-arms but also in depictions of landscapes and human figures. On the upper floor the workbenches and instruments once used by the craftsmen can be admired.

One of the city's main museums is the ★ **Galleria dell'Accademia** ❺❽ (weekdays except Monday 9am–2pm, Sunday and public holidays 9am–1pm), which contains important collections of sculpture and paintings. Michelangelo's *Slaves*, his *Pietà* and also his world-famous ★★★ *David* (it used to stand in front of the Palazzo Vecchio but was replaced by a copy in 1910) are just three of the main attractions here. The *Slaves* (1519, unfinished) were originally destined for the tomb of Pope Julius II, and they evoke Michelangelo's unique concept, expressed in his poetry, that the sculpture already exists within the block of stone, and that it is the sculptor's job merely to remove what is superfluous. The *Pietà* from Palestrina near Rome is not now thought to be by him, but the colossal statue of *David* established Michelangelo as the foremost sculptor of his time at the age of 26.

The Accademia also has a picture gallery, containing many fine examples of 14th- and 15th-century Tuscan painting (Paolo Uccello, Orcagna, Taddeo Gaddi, Botticelli, etc) as well as work by 16th-century Tuscan Mannerists (Pontormo, Allori, Bronzino).

The Via Ricasoli emerges into the Piazza San Marco, where the **University** ❺❾ is situated. This part of the city is always full of students. **San Marco** ❻⓿, with its church, monastery and museum, is a favourite with art-lovers from all over the world. The church, however, is the least interesting bit: despite dating back to 1299, it suffered from alterations during the 17th and 18th centuries and lost its architectural uniqueness in 1780 when it was given its neoclassical facade. Worthy of note inside the church are a crucifix in the style of Giotto (14th-century), the *Baldachin Madonna* by Fra Bartolomeo on the second altar on the right (1509), and at the next altar the *Madonna in Prayer*, an 8th-century Roman mosaic (705–7). The Cappella di Sant'Antonino contains the tomb of St Antonino of Florence (1389–1459), who as archbishop was responsible for the construction of the new monastery next door. Cosimo the Elder (a rich banker with a guilty conscience) paid for the new monastery, and Michelozzo built it between 1437 and 1452. The new occupants were Dominican monks from Fiesole, and their disciplined, ascetic lifestyle is reflected in the architecture. Savonarola (*see page 11*) also came from this monastery.

Michelozzo's building, the first Renaissance monastery, is sober and severe in contrast to the formal exuberance of his contemporary Brunelleschi – discipline and asceticism forbade pure decoration. An austere form of architecture thus developed which eschewed all that was in any way superficial – just the right environment for the paintings by the artist-monk Fra Beato Angelico. San Marco is virtually his museum. His real name was Fra Giovanni, and he lived from 1385 to 1455. After moving from the heights of Fiesole down to Florence he was commissioned by St Antonino to do the frescoes for the new building.

The entrance to the ★★ **Museo di San Marco** (Tuesday–Saturday 9am–2pm, Sunday and public holidays 9am–1pm) is next to the church.

Museo di San Marco: Crucifixion and Saints by Beato Angelico

Ground floor

1 Entrance from the piazza, and vestibule
2 Cloister of St Antonino, by Michelozzo; the lunettes with scenes from the life of the saint were added much later and detract from the originally very austere and meditative effect
3 Above the church door, Beato Angelico's lunette of *St Peter Martyr* enjoining silence
4 *St Dominic at the Foot of the Cross* (Beato Angelico)
5 Sala del Capitolo. *St Dominic with the Rule of the Order*; for discipline to be maintained, monks had to accept punishment here. *Crucifixion and Saints*; Christ as Redeemer (Beato Angelico)
6 Sala del Lavabo. Above the door, a *Pietà* by Beato Angelico; *Madonna with St Anne and Saints* (Fra Bartolomeo)
7 Refettorio Grande. Frescoes from the Fra Bartolomeo school
8 Above the door to the Hospice: *Christ as a Pilgrim* (Beato Angelico)

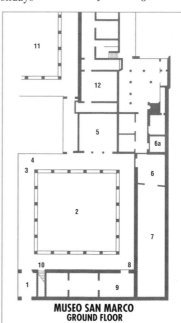

MUSEO SAN MARCO
GROUND FLOOR

Savanarola by Fra Bartolomeo

Michelozzo's Library

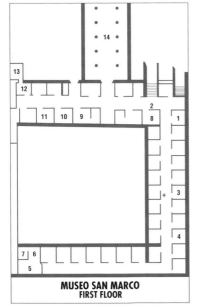

MUSEO SAN MARCO
FIRST FLOOR

9 Ospizio dei Pellegrini. Exhibition of tablets by Beatro Angelico; on the front wall one of his main works *The Descent from the Cross* (1435)

10 Above the door *Thomas of Aquino* (Beatro Angelico)

11 Chiostro di San Domenico by Michelozzo; the arcades contain material salvaged after the demolition of the Ghetto and the Mercato Vecchio in the 19th century to make way for the Piazza della Repubblica

12 Refettorio Piccolo. *The Last Supper* by Ghirlandaio (1480–90)

13 *The Last Judgement* by Fra Bartolomeo

First floor

The Dormitory beneath the huge wooden roof consists of 44 small monastic cells, each with their own vault and adorned with an intimate fresco (by Beato Angelico), of which the following is a selection.

1 *Jesus Appears to Mary*

2 *Annunciation* (one of Fra Angelico's most famous works)

3 *Transfiguration*

4 *Coronation of the Virgin*

5 Prior's room, where Savonarola also lived; his portrait was painted by his supporter Fra Bartolomeo

6 Savonarola's cell

7 Savonarola's sleeping chamber with the banner he always carried when preaching

8 Cell of St Antonino

9 Cell of Beato Angelico

10 *Prayer on the Mount of Olives with Madonna and St Martha*

11 *Communion of the Apostles*

12/13 Cosimo the Elder retired to these cells

14 Library by Michelozzo, the first one of the Renaissance

From the Piazza San Marco, the Via XXVII Aprile leads to the former convent of ★ **Sant' Appollonia** ❻❶ (opening hours Tuesday–Saturday 9am–2pm, Sunday and public holidays 9am–1pm), where the ★★ *Last Supper* fresco by Andrea del Castagno (1445–50) can be admired in the refectory; it reveals the influence of Masaccio's pictorial illusionism and Castagno's use of perspective.

On the Via Cavour, which runs past the church of San Marco, house numbers 55, 57 and 59 are all taken up by an impressive building, the **Casino Mediceo** ❻❷; the 11-bay facade was devised by Bernardo Buontalenti (1536–1608).

On the same side of the street, at No 69, is the modest entrance to the **Chiostro dello Scalzo**  (opening hours Monday, Thursday 9am–1pm). Andrea del Sarto (1468–1530) painted a cycle of monochrome frescoes in stages here on the *Life of St John the Baptist* and also *Allegories of the Virtues* (two panels have been attributed to his workshop).

Piazza SS Annunziata

Assuming it is not closed for lunch, the ★ **Farmacia** over the road at No 146r is also a very rewarding place to visit; it has a magnificent painted ceiling and some fine glazed terracotta decoration.

Anyone keen on taking a break at this point will find Florence's botanical garden, the **Giardino dei Semplici** (note the opening hours: Monday, Wednesday, Friday 9am–noon only), around the next corner just a few steps away from the pharmacy. It was laid out by order of Cosimo I in 1545.

In the Giardino dei Semplici

The Via Giorgio La Pira, on which the Giardino dei Semplici lies, comes out into the Piazza San Marco, where a left-turn down the Via Cesare Battisti leads to the ★ **Piazza SS Annunziata**, designed by Brunelleschi, and surrounded on three sides by porticoes. It is the most beautiful square in Florence. The loggia of Brunelleschi's ★ **Spedale degli Innocenti** (Foundling Hospital, 1421) inspired Antonio Sangallo to build the portico arch in front of the church opposite; the equestrian statue of Grand Duke Ferdinand I was designed by Giambologna and executed in 1608 by Pietro Tacca, who also contributed the two ★ **fountains** (1629).

SS Annunziata: the atrium

Behind the portico of the church of **SS Annunziata** lies an atrium with frescoes showing *Scenes from the Life of the Virgin*, and also early works by Andrea del Sarto (*Birth* and *Arrival of the Three Magi*, the latter with the artist's self-portrait in the right-hand corner). The atrium was designed by Michelozzo, who rebuilt the entire

The gilt ceiling

Interior detail

complex in 1444. It was the only part of the complex to survive the later structural changes; the addition of a **gilt ceiling** (1669), baroque decoration, ex-votos and works of art during the centuries that followed simply interfered with the original architectural clarity. What remains of the restructuring during the 15th century is by no means harmonious. Michelozzo's centralised design, inspired by antique models, was continued by Leon Battista Alberti despite fierce resistance: the rotunda was completed in the year 1477.

Works of art (a selection): left of the entrance, a large circular tribune (designed by Michelozzo, 1461) with a fresco of the *Coronation of the Virgin* in the cupola; the fresco of *St Julian and the Saviour* in the first chapel on the left, and the fresco of the *Trinity* in the second chapel to the left are both by Andrea del Castagno (c 1455). The Chiostro dei Morti (Cloister of the Dead) is entered from the door in the north transept: fresco of ★ *Madonna del Sacco* (The Madonna with the Sack), the most famous work by Andrea del Sarto (1525), is over the door. At the end of the cloister on the left is the Cappella di San Luca, or 'Artists' Chapel', which has belonged to the Accademia delle Arti del Disegno since 1565; many famous artists lie buried here, including Pontormo (1567) and Benvenuto Cellini.

Begun in 1421, Filippo Brunelleschi's ★ **Foundling Hospital** (Spedale degli Innocenti) ❻❼ is the very first building in Renaissance form. Brunelleschi (1377–1446) had been studying the architecture of the Tuscan Romanesque or proto-Renaissance, which he believed to represent the architecture of Antiquity. Commissioned by the

The Foundling Hospital

Arte della Seta (silk guild), he employed a variety of proto-Renaissance motifs to create a formal language for the Early Renaissance. He never imitated, though: instead, he took ideas and developed them anew. Unlike his cathedral dome, whose construction and shape is distinctly Gothic in character, the Foundling Hospital facade is a work of a completely different kind, consisting of a colonnade on the ground floor with slender Corinthian columns and wide semicircular arches, and a first floor with generously spaced rectangular windows under shallow pediments corresponding directly to the arches beneath. Medallions in coloured terracotta by Andrea della Robbia – the famous babes in swaddling clothes sold in cheap copies of all sizes by the souvenir-dealers in Florence – are placed into the spandrels of the arcade. While the motifs may well all be Roman, the slenderness of the columns in particular lends the facade an expression as different from a building like the Colosseum as from any Gothic arcade.

*Medallion by
Andrea della Robbia*

The art gallery here contains a fine *Coronation of the Virgin* by Nero di Bicci (15th-century) and also the magnificent *Adoration of the Magi* by Ghirlandaio (1488).

Spread out along the Via della Colonna is the ★ **Museo Archeologico** ⓰ (Tuesday–Saturday 9am–2pm, Sunday and public holidays 9am–1pm). The collections here concentrate on Greek–Roman Antiquity, ancient Egypt and also the Etruscans.

*Exhibits in the
Museo Archeologico*

At No 58, Borgo Pinti, the second street to intersect the Via della Colonna after the museum, an inconspicuous-looking door leads the way to one of the most magnificent frescoes in the whole city, in the convent of ★ **Santa Maria Maddalena de'Pazzi** ⓱. An atrium lined with pillars leads into the church itself, which dates back to 1257. It underwent several alterations over the centuries, and is a fine example of Florentine baroque. The trapezoid windows are a typical feature, as is the presbytery, completed in 1685: the golden and reddish tones of the main altar stand out against the dark marble floor. Cupola frescoes (Piero Dandini) and paintings with *Scenes from the Life of the Virgin* (Luca Giordano) complete the harmonious scene.

On the right before the presbytery, signposted passageways lead to the former chapter house, which contains a ★★ **fresco** of the *Crucifixion* by Perugino (daily 9am–12noon and 5–7pm; donation). The clarity and magnificence of the fresco (1493–5) are immediately striking: the ample sculpturesque figures are gracefully posed; the harmonious space is tightly controlled in the foreground and middle ground, while the background gives the impression of infinite space.

From the Borgo Pinti, the route continues down the Via dei Pilastri, a small street with lots of little shops; the Via

The Synagogue

The Loggia del Pesce

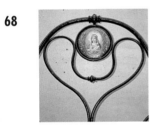

Mercato delle Pulci: bargain offers

Farini joins this street from the left, and contains the **Synagogue** (Tempio Israelitico) **70**, built in the Hispano-Moresque style between 1874 and 1882. This centralised structure with its tall green dome is particularly striking because of its wealth of decoration, making it reminiscent of a mosque – or of San Marco in Venice.

The Via dei Pilastri leads directly to the piazza and the church of **Sant'Ambrogio** **71**, one of the oldest churches in Florence, containing the tombs of sculptors Mino da Fiesole (1430–84) and Andrea Verrocchio (1435–88). The left-hand side-chapel contains a marble *Tabernacle* by Mino, with terracotta angels from the Della Robbia school; the church's historic facade can be seen on a processional fresco dating from 1486.

The Via Pietrapiana now heads straight back towards the city centre, past the **Loggia del Pesce** **72**, now reconstructed on this spot. Vasari built it as a fish market in 1567, but it had to make way for the Piazza della Repubblica in the 19th century. Beyond the loggia there is now a very lively and picturesque ★ **Mercato delle Pulci** (flea market) with fixed booths, where all sorts of bargains can still be found, whether books, furniture or antiques.

The continuation of the Via Pietrapiana towards the city centre is the Via dell'Oriuolo, which passes the museum called **'Firenze com'era'** ('Florence as it once was') **73** (daily except Thursday 9am–2pm, Sunday and public holidays 8am–1pm). This former convent houses pictures, engravings and drawings of Florence from medieval times to the present. The Via dell'Oriuolo then emerges back at the starting point of the route, the Piazza del Duomo.

★★★ Duomo – Santa Maria degli Angeli – Santa Maria Nuova – Arco San Piero – Via Ghibellina – ★ Casa Buonarotti – ★★ Santa Croce – Ponte alle Grazie – Porta San Niccolò – ★★ Piazzale Michelangelo – ★★ San Miniato al Monte

The Via dei Servi leaves the Piazza del Duomo on the northeastern side of the cathedral (opposite the left transept), and at its junction with the Via dei Pucci the Medici coat-of-arms can be seen, with its seven balls. The next turn-off to the right, the Via del Castellaccio, opens out into the Piazza Brunelleschi, with the round church of **Santa Maria degli Angeli** *(Rotonda Brunelleschi)* **74**.

Santa Maria degli Angeli

After returning from Rome in 1433, Brunelleschi designed this octagonal building as the first centralised structure of the Renaissance, but it was never completed. Today it is used as a language laboratory by the university.

The Via degli Alfani intersects with the Via della Pergola, which contains the theatre of the same name. The Via della Pergola then joins the Via Sant'Egidio, and from here **Santa Maria Nuova** **75**, the oldest hospital in the city, with its 17th-century arcades and busts of the Medici, is just a few steps away. It was founded in 1286.

Strolling in the Borgo degli Albizi

At the other end of the Via Sant'Egidio is a small square with an arched entrance, the **Arco di San Piero** **76**, beyond which there is a fine view of the city's picturesque towers and roofs. A small vegetable market and several shops and restaurants cater busily to the needs of this very lively quarter. The narrow **Borgo degli Albizi** is a good place for a stroll.

At the second crossroads the Via Matteo Palmieri joins the **Via Ghibellina**; to the left on the corner is the 14th-century **Palazzo Quaratesi** **77**, and a few metres further on to the right is the **Palazzo Borghese** **78**. This gigantic neoclassical building has 21 bays – a Florentine record. The projecting central section is adorned by two symmetrical wings. In the opposite direction on the left is the **★ Casa Buonarotti** **79** (weekdays except Tuesday 9.30am–1.30pm, Sunday and public holidays 9.30am–1.30pm), which Michelangelo bought for a nephew and where the Buonarotti family lived until their line died out in 1858. Today the house is a museum, currently being reorganised. In the vestibule to the right of the entrance hall is a fine bronze *head of Michelangelo* by Daniele da Volterra. The room to the left at the top of the stairs contains two early works: the *Madonna of the Steps*, a marble bas-relief, supposedly the artist's first ever sculpture, and *Battle of the Centaurs* (1492), carved just before the death of Lorenzo the Magnificent and left unfinished.

Casa Buonarotti

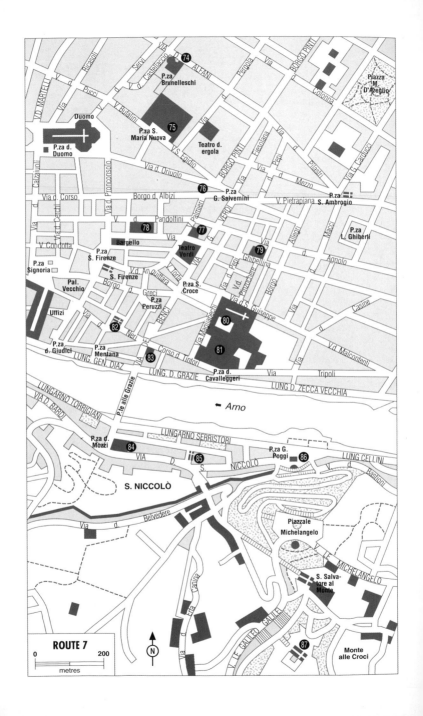

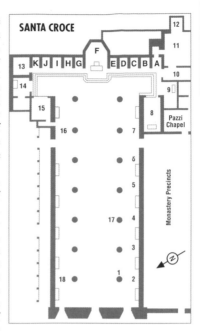

The Via delle Pinzochere leads to the colonnade on the northern side of ★★ **Santa Croce** ⑩, Florence's Franciscan church. The present building was begun in 1294 by Arnolfo di Cambio, and construction work continued until 1442. The facade and the campanile date from the 19th century, and their magnificent marble contrasts sharply with the intentionally simple brickwork of the original structure. Santa Croce was the scene of the Pazzi conspiracy against the Medici in 1478.

The bright, 115-m (380-ft) long, three-aisled interior is lined by solemn arcades of pointed arches, and has an open timber roof. The main altar is emphasised by the polygonal apse and the stained-glass windows. The wealth of art treasures in this church and its sheer architectural magnificence (despite encroachments by Vasari in the 16th century) make Santa Croce one of the most popular sights in Florence, and it was chosen as a last resting place by many of the city's inhabitants. The floor alone has 276 tomb-slabs, and there are tombs of many famous people in the side-aisles.

Santa Croce facade

Michelangelo's tomb

Right-hand side-aisle

1 *Madonna del Latte* by Antonio Rossellino (1427–70)
2 Tomb of Michelangelo carved by Vasari (1564).
3 Cenotaph to Dante by Stefano Ricci (1829); Dante is buried in Ravenna
4 Tomb of the poet Vittorio Alfieri by Canova (1810)
5 Tomb of the politician and poet Niccolò Machiavelli (1469–1527) by Innocenzo Spinazzi (1787)
6 *Annunciation*, Donatello's masterpiece in gilded limestone; to the left of it is the tomb of humanist Leonardo Bruni (1369–1444), one of the most influential sepulchral monuments of the Renaissance, by Bernardo Rossellino
7 Tomb of the composer Gioacchino Rossini (1792–1868) by Giuseppe Cassioli (1886); left of the altar is the tomb of poet Ugo Foscolo (1939)
8 Cappella Castellani with fresco cycle by Agnolo Gaddi (c 1383)
9 Cappella Baroncelli. The *Madonna and Child* in the lunette on the Baroncelli tomb has been attributed to Taddeo Gaddi (father of Agnolo) who also did the four *prophets* above it; the altarpiece of the *Coronation of the Virgin* is by Giotto and workshop. On the right wall is the *Madonna of the Girdle*, a fresco by

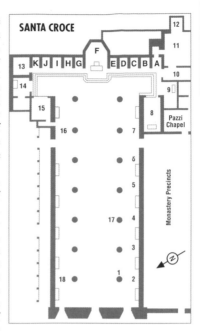

Bardi Chapel: Giotto's Life of St Francis
Gothic stained glass

Bastiano Mainardi (late 15th-century), and on the other walls, more frescoes by Giotto's pupil Taddeo Gaddi: *Scenes from the Life of the Virgin* (1332–8)

10 Sacristy Corridor by Michelozzo, with Gothic windows

11 Sacristy (14th-century), containing fresco of the *Passion* by Niccolò Gerini (c 1380); valuable intarsia furniture by Giovanni di Michele (c 1454); *Crucifixion* by Taddeo Gaddi

12 Cappella Rinuccini with Gothic wrought-iron grille (1371) and frescoes showing *Scenes from the Life of the Virgin* (left) *and St Mary Magdalen* (right), by Giovanni da Milano and workshop; polyptych by Giovanni del Biondo (1379)

Choir chapels

Florentine families filled the chapels in the transept on either side of the main altar with works of art.

A Cappella Velluti with damaged frescoes of the *Archangel Michael*, possibly by Cimabue

B Cappella Calderini, rebuilt by Gherardo Silvani (c 1640); damaged vault painting by Giovanni di San Giovanni (1621)

C Cappella Bonaparte (Giugni) with tombs of the Bonaparte family (19th-century)

D Cappella Peruzzi with ★★ **frescoes** by Giotto in his mature period (c 1320): on the left wall, *Scenes from the Life of John the Baptist*, and on the right wall, *Scenes from the Life of St John the Evangelist*

E Cappella Bardi with more ★★ **frescoes** by Giotto (c 1317) including *The Life of St Francis*; ★ **Altarpiece** of St Francis and 20 *Scenes from his Life* by Barone Berlinghieri (13th-century)

F Cappella Maggiore (sanctuary) with frescoes by Agnolo Gaddi (c 1380): *Legend of the Cross*; polyptych of *Madonna and Saints* by Niccolò Gerini and workshop; crucifix by the 'Master of Figline'; stained-glass lancet windows by Agnolo Gaddi

G Cappella Tosinghi e Spinelli with an *Assumption of the Virgin* by the 'Master of Figline'; altarpiece by Giovanni del Biondo (1372)

H Cappella della Madre Italiana, dedicated to the mothers of those who died in World War I (Libero Andreotti, 1926)

I Cappella Ricasoli containing *St Antonio of Padua* by Luigi Sabatelli and workshop (1840)

J Cappella Pulci with frescoes by Bernardo Daddi and workshop (c 1330): *Martyrdom of St Lawrence and St Stephen*; terracotta altar by Giovanni della Robbia (early 16th-century)

K Cappella Bardi di Vernio with frescoes by Maso di Banco (c 1340): *Life of St Sylvester*; altarpiece by Giovanni del Biondo; in the larger niche to the left a *Last Judgement* attributed to Maso di Banco; in the smaller one a *Deposition* attributed to Taddeo Gaddi (14th-century)

Stoning of St Stephen

Left-hand side-aisle

13 Cappella Niccolini, designed by Giovanni Antonio Dosio (1579–85), with paintings by Allessandro Allori (1588). It was here that Stendhal experienced the surfeit of beauty that came to be known as 'Stendhal's Syndrome'

14 Cappella Bardi containing the wooden crucifix by Donatello (c 1425) which Brunelleschi thought resembled a peasant; he then carved his own crucifix for Santa Maria Novella

15 Cappella Salviati with the *Martyrdom of St Lawrence* by Jacopo Ligozzi (c 1600); to the left of the entrance is the tomb (1869) of composer Luigi Cherubini (1760–1842)

16 Tomb of Carlo Marsuppini (1398–1453) by Desiderio da Settignano, who drew inspiration from Rossellino's Bruni tomb opposite

17 Pulpit by Benedetto da Maiano (1472–76) with delicately carved *Scenes from the Life of St Francis*

18 Tomb (1737) of Galileo Galilei (1574–1642)

Before leaving the church, take a look at the rose window in the west front with its *Deposition* by Giovanni del Ponte (15th-century). In front of the church, turn left and enter the **cloister**: its harmonious arches betray the identity of its designer – Brunelleschi. At the end of it is one of his greatest works, even though he never completed

In the cloister

The Pazzi Chapel

The interior of the cupola

Calcio in costume

it: the ★★ **Pazzi Chapel** (Cappella de' Pazzi). It was begun in 1443 and finished 15 years after Brunelleschi's death in 1461. A hemispherical dome covers a central square, which is extended on either side so that the square forms the centre of a rectangle. The minor spatial compartment, opening off a third side of the main square, is a corresponding square apse covered by a dome and containing the altar. The frieze above the capitals is adorned with angel heads by Desiderio di Settignano; the creamy wall surface is marked off in geometric patterns by dark grey stone; the polychrome enamelled terracotta is from the della Robbia workshop (*see page 86*). The pendentives of the cupola contain polychrome roundels of the Evangelists, looking down at the enamelled terracotta roundels of the seated Apostles. This chapel is a masterpiece of the Florentine Renaissance.

Directly opposite, in the refectory, is the **Museo dell'Opera di Santa Croce ㉛** (daily except Wednesday 10am–12.30pm and 2.30–6.30pm, in winter 10am–12.30pm and 3–5pm.) This museum houses the world-famous ★★★ *Crucifix* by Cimabue which has now been restored after it was almost completely destroyed in the 1966 flood. The fresco on the end wall is by Taddeo Gaddi, and includes *The Tree of The Cross* and a *Last Supper*. Donatello's colossal bronze of *St Louis* is also here, as is Orcagna's *Triumph of Death*. Further fragments of frescoes can be viewed in the main hall and the rooms adjoining it.

The Piazza Santa Croce used to be a popular venue for public gatherings and tournaments; it was also where the historic football match called the Calcio was played – and lost by the German occupiers – during the Carnival of 1530. Today, the statue of Dante (1865) has had to be shifted from the centre to the side of the piazza to make way for the annual *calcio in costume*. The south-

ern side of the square has some interesting *sporti*, those projecting upper floors that are so characteristic of Florence; in the year 1619 house No 22, the Palazzo dell'Antella, was provided with its colourful decoration in just 20 days by a team of 12 artists under the supervision of Giovanni di San Giovanni.

The other end of the square opposite the church is where the Via Torta (Crooked Street) begins; the route follows the Via dell'Isola delle Stinche, then the Via dei Bentaccordi as far as the Piazza dei Peruzzi, and then goes past some of the oldest buildings in the city and on to the Via de'Benci. This last street has to be followed around to the right, and just after it starts to widen, the mighty 13th-century Casa-Torre Alberti, a typical old Florentine family tower, can be seen on the left-hand side. This tower belonged to the family of architect Leon Battista Alberti (*see page 87*); its inviting-looking loggia was added in the early 15th century.

At the next intersection it's worth taking a small detour to the right, down the Via de' Neri to the church of ★ San Remigio ㉜, consecrated to St Remigius (Saint-Rémy) of Reims. After the simple facade the French Gothic three-aisled interior comes as quite a surprise (13th to 14th-century): it has dichromatic pointed-arch arcades, and a ribbed vault. The most striking fresco here is the *Madonna Enthroned*, attributed to the Cimabue school (13th-century).

Right at the intersection on the way back to the Via de'Benci lies the **Museo della Fondazione Horne** ㉝ (weekdays 9am–1pm, closed Sunday), presented to Florence by the English art historian Herbert Percy Horne (1864–1916). This collection of painting, sculpture and historic furniture contains a fine *St Stephen* attributed to Giotto, and also a book containing sketches by Tiepolo (18th-century).

From the Via de'Benci, the **Ponte alle Grazie** leads across the Arno and into the San Niccolò quarter; on the left-hand side of the Piazza de'Mozzi stands the **Museo Bardini** ㉞ (dailiy except Wednesday 9am–2pm, Sunday and public holidays 8am–1pm), built in the 19th century, which contains large collections of sculpture, paintings and tapestries.

The pretty Via di San Niccolò leads past the church of **San Niccolò sopr'Arno** ㉟ – Michelangelo hid from the German occupiers in its campanile in 1530 – and then comes out at the **Porta San Niccolò** ㊱, a tower from the city's third wall, dating from 1324 and still its original size. Winding steps now lead up to the ★★**Piazzale Michelangelo**, a viewing platform opened in 1875; a copy of Michelangelo's *David* is surrounded here by copies of the *Four Seasons* from the Medici Chapels.

Piazzale Michelangelo: souvenirs and view

San Miniato al Monte

Past the restaurant loggia at the back, steps lead to the church of San Salvatore al Monte by Cronaca (1475), which Michelangelo used to call his *bella villanella* (pretty country maid), and then up to ★★ **San Miniato al Monte** ❽, one of the oldest churches in the city. A building stood on this site in the 4th century. The present structure was started in 1018, and is a fine example of Florentine Romanesque architecture; the formal language and the materials used are very reminiscent of the Baptistry. The facade of the church is decorative: its five arches bear no relation to the three-aisled basilica inside. Only the top section, with the triangular gable, is the same width as the nave; the sloping diagonals at the sides iron out the architectural contradiction.

The interior with its open timber roof is lent rhythm by alternating groups of columns, drawing the eye towards the mosaic of Christ in the apse. Just before the magnificent rood screen is the elegant ★ **Cappella del Crocifisso**, a tiny vaulted temple with pillars, terracotta and paintings – Michelozzo worked here together with Luca della Robbia, and the paintings are by Agnolo Gaddi (1394–6). Another successful Florentine joint venture was the Cappella del Cardinale di Portogallo (left aisle). On the ground plan of a Greek cross, Brunelleschi's pupil Manetti built this funeral chapel (1461–6) for the Cardinal of Lisbon, who died in Florence; the ceiling has five medallions by Luca della Robbia, and the frescoes are by Alesso Baldovinetti. The Gothic sacristy (approached from the choir) contains a *Life of St Benedict* fresco by Spinello Aretino (late 14th-century). The 11th-century ★ **Crypt**, which houses the relics of St Minias, is the most important part of the building. The narrow Byzantine windows in the nave and the dichromatic marble are both characteristic features of Florentine Romanesque.

76

Interior frescoes

The interior with its open timber roof

Excursions

1. Fiesole

Take bus No 7 via Stazione-Duomo-San Marco 7km/4 miles); car drivers should leave the city centre at the Piazza della Libertà and travel along the Via Don Giovanni Minzoni. Just outside the city is San Domenico with its church and convent (founded 1406), where Fra Beato Angelico, the painter-monk, used to live; when the convent took over San Marco down in the city he was given an important task (*see page 63*). The convent church, altered in the 17th century and equipped with an elegant atrium (1635), contains a *Madonna with Angels and Saints* by Fra Angelico (c 1430) in the first side-chapel on the left; the architectural background was added by Lorenzo di Credi in 1501. The chapter house of the convent contains a *Crucifixion* fresco by Fra' Angelico (c 1440).

Badia Fiesolana

At the traffic lights, the road goes left in the direction of **Badia Fiesolana** (Fiesole Abbey). It was probably built on the site of the martyrium of St Romulus. For four centuries, from 1028 until 1437, it was a Benedictine house. The unfinished facade still dates from the 11th century, and its dichromatic marble is reminiscent of the Baptistry and San Miniato. Otherwise, the church and convent are Renaissance structures; Cosimo the Elder had them altered, Brunelleschi-style, after 1437, and he turned the Badia Fiesolana into a meeting-place for artists and scholars. The convent buildings today house the European University Institute, and those lucky enough to live and work here have breathtaking views of Florence.

77

The road then winds away from San Domenico and uphill to the Piazza of **Fiesole** (Roman *Faesulae*), an Etruscan city. Archaeological remains have been found here dating back to the 7th century BC, and under the Roman Empire the town was given a capitol, a theatre and thermal baths. It was only in 1125 that Florence finally succeeded in annexing its neighbour. The campanile dominating the piazza is reminiscent of the one on the Palazzo Vecchio; in fact it dates from 1213, and the one in Florence was modelled after it. Behind its rather unattractive facade, the cathedral of **San Romolo** contains a three-aisled, bare stone interior dating back to 1028; it was altered in the 13th century. The raised choir lies above the hall crypt, with its archaic capitals and columns. The Cappella Salutati (on the right-hand side of the presbytery) contains some fine work by Mino da Fiesole (c 1431–84), and the large altarpiece above the high altar is by Bicci di Lorenzo (1450).

San Romolo: interior views

Opposite the facade is the Bishop's Palace, to the left of which a very steep, paved lane leads up to the site of the Etruscan and later Roman acropolis. On the way up there

The view from Fiesole

The church of San Francisco

Teatro Romano

are some superb views of Florence. The lane goes past the 6th-century church of San Alessandro, built on the site of a Bacchic temple. The marble columns of this three-aisled building are Roman.

At the very top of the hill, on the site of the former acropolis, stand the convent buildings of **San Francesco**. The simple little church with its single aisle and vaulted ceiling contains several fine 15th-century paintings. A steep flight of steps leads down to the Missionary Museum, which has a collection of Etruscan and Roman (as well as Egyptian and Chinese) exhibits.

Archaeological excavations at Fiesole
Behind the cathedral is the Museo Bandini (terracotta of the della Robbia school, panels of the Tuscan school, 14th to 15th-century), and beyond the museum is the **Teatro Romano** (Roman Theatre, daily except Tuesday 9am–7pm, in winter 9am–6pm).

The structure here once held around 25,000 spectators, and it is one of the oldest Roman theatres (1st-century BC). The raised stage, 26m (85ft) wide, can be easily made out. Further down the hill the remains of some Roman baths have been excavated; there are chambers of varying sizes, including a room where the water was heated, dating from the time of Hadrian (117–138). To the left of the theatre is a temple area, with remains of a Roman temple and also a mighty Etruscan one (3rd-century BC). Across the whole area is a long Etruscan city-wall; its impressive, rough-hewn masonry contrasts with the more finely-structured Roman walls.

All the finds dating from Etrusco-Roman times (ceramics, coins, statues, sculpture, architectural fragments) are on display in the Museo Civico here and also in the Antiquarium Costatini, to the right of the theatre.

2. Sesto Fiorentino (★ Etruscan graves)

The No 28 bus leaves from the station square *(Stazione)* for Sesto Fiorentino (get off at La Mula); car drivers need to leave the ring road at the Piazza Costituzione and then follow signs to Sesto Fiorentino. Roughly 1km (½ mile) after entering it on the Via Antonio Gramsci, the Via degli Strozzi branches off (yellow signpost saying *tombe etrusche*); right next to the first turn-off on the right is **La Mula** (opening hours 16 April–30 September: Tuesday 10am–12noon, Saturday 10am–12noon and 5–6.30pm; 1 October–15 April: Saturday only, 10am–12noon). A privately-owned strip of land provides access here to the Etruscan burial chamber *(tholos)*. A flight of steps leads 18m (60ft) underground, and beyond the portal, which consists of three stone monoliths, the round burial chamber opens out. It is 9m (30ft) in diameter. The walls consist of rough-hewn stones; the chamber tapers as it gets higher, as far as the surface stone on top. Despite the fact that this room was used for food storage for centuries (9m/30ft below ground the temperature remains the same) there is no doubt that it dates from Etruscan times (7th to 6th-century BC) and was built as a burial chamber.

The way to the Etruscan graves

The Via degli Strozzi comes out into a main road; on the left at house No 95 is the entrance to **La Montagnola** (opening hours: in summer Saturday, Sunday and public holidays 10am–1pm and 5–7pm, Tuesday, Thursday 10am–1pm; in winter Saturday, Sunday and public holidays 10am–1pm).

The 14-m (45-ft) long and 2-m (7-ft) wide corridor *(dromos)* leading to the portal – also made of three monoliths – has survived the millennia (7th to 6th-century BC). Beyond the portal a somewhat narrower, covered passageway leads to the burial chambers. Two smallish chambers (3m x 1.5m/10ft x 5ft) lie on either side of the passageway, which then emerges into the main chamber, which is roughly 5m (16ft) deep. At its centre, a 5-m (16-ft) high tuff pillar rises up to the pseudo-cupola above; the stones of the walls here are more finely-worked than those in the passageway. This burial mound was first discovered in 1959; it had been filled with debris since Roman times. Tomb robbers got here first, though: only fragments remain of the burial gifts.

3. Prato

Numerous trains travel to the town of Prato (20km/13 miles) from the main station *(Stazione)*; buses run by the firm of Lazzi also do direct trips, and leave from the right-hand side of the station. Car drivers should take the A1 *(Autosole)* in the direction of Bologna as far as the exit to Prato, or the country road via Sesto Fiorentino *(see Excursion 2)*. The area around Prato (which means

The outdoor pulpit

*Romanesque arches
of the cathedral facade*

meadow) has been inhabited since Palaeolithic times. During the Middle Ages Prato was an independent city-state with its own flourishing textile and silk industries, until it was swallowed up by Florence in 1351. The town remained wealthy despite this, however, as evidenced by the magnificent works of art to be found here. Prato also has a famous son: Francesco di Marco Datini (died 1410) was an Italian international merchant and banker whose business and private papers, preserved here in Prato constitute one of the most important archives of the economic history of the Middle Ages.

From the station a bus travels to the Piazza Duomo, where the bus from Florence arrives (parking available). All that remains of the original 12th-century ★ **Cathedral of Santo Stefano** are the campanile and the cloister; the facade in dichromatic marble was only built in 1385, though the exterior arcades date from 1211. The ★★ **outdoor pulpit** on the facade is an architectural rarity; it is where the *Sacro Cingolo*, or Holy Girdle, is venerated five times annually (Easter, 1 May, 15 August, 8 September, and Christmas). Donatello did some fine marble reliefs for the balustrade (1434–8), and the pulpit itself is by Michelozzo (the original parapet is in the Cathedral Museum, *see page 81*).

The ★ **campanile** is also worth a closer look: because of the extension work during the 13th century it is now jammed between the nave and transept, and the original way through it via the ground floor had to be walled up. Above are three Romanesque double-mullioned windows *(bifore)* and above them, two far more eye-catching storeys; the top one is Gothic (1340–56) while the lower

one, which used to be the belfry, has had its decoration adapted but its Romanesque arches retained. It is this combination that gives the campanile of Prato Cathedral its unique appearance.

Doorway to the cathedral

The interior, with its dichromatic accentuation of the arches, was certainly a novelty at the time it was built (1211). The cup-shaped ★ **marble pulpit** is by Mino da Fiesole and Antonio Rossellino (1473); Mino designed it and did two of the skilfully carved scenes (*Banquet of Herod* and *Martyrdom of St John the Baptist)*, Rossellino did the other scenes and the workshop took care of the fine sculpture at the base of the pulpit.

The transept is a Gothic extension attributed to Giovanni Pisano (as are the extra storeys on the campanile), and was completed in 1317. The presbytery contains one of the finest ★ **fresco cycles** of the early Renaissance: Filippo Lippi painted the ★ *Life of St John the Baptist* here and designed the stained-glass windows between 1452 and 1466; the banquet scene with the guests wearing costumes from Lippi's time and the graceful Salome is justly famous.

The cathedral also contains ★ **frescoes** by Paolo Uccello and Agnolo Gaddi, as well as sculpture by Giovanni Pisano, Benedetto da Maiano, Ferdinando Tacca, and many others.

81

To the left of the facade is the entrance to the Cathedral Museum, or ★ **Museo dell'Opera del Duomo**, which contains Donatello's original dancing *putti* for the outdoor pulpit, as well as frescoes, liturgical objects and altar panels. The inner courtyard provides access to the former ★ **cloister**, one side of which has been preserved in its entirety: with its polychrome marble, elegant capitals and finely-structured appearance as a whole, the cloister is a rare example of the Byzantine-Romanesque style in Tuscany (late 12th-century). There is access from here to the interesting ★ **crypt**.

A rest from sightseeing

On the site of the mighty *fortezza* that Frederick II Hohenstaufen had built here in 1248 (Prato was friendly to the emperor) stands a rather unprepossessing square structure, with a round roof and lantern above its unfinished exterior – **Santa Maria delle Carceri**.

The ★ **interior**, however, is one of the main works of the Renaissance period and is by Giuliano da Sangallo (1484–92). This centralised, domed building in the shape of a Greek cross is reminiscent of Brunelleschi's Pazzi Chapel in Florence. A continuous balustrade runs around the wall; pilasters, circles and semicircles and the classic contrast between light and dark stone all contribute to the austerity of this interior, which is rounded off perfectly by colourful enamelled terracotta of the della Robbia school.

IERVSALEM

Art History

Opposite:
The Gates of Paradise

Archaeological finds have proved that the region occupied by present-day Florence was inhabited before the Roman colony was founded: impressive monuments testifying to the fact include the well-preserved Etruscan tombs La Montagnola and La Mula near Sesto Fiorentino (*see page 79*). The exhibits in the city's Museo Archeologico document the finds from Roman *Florentia*. From the Middle Ages onwards, Florence developed its own very individual style of architecture.

Teatro Romano at Fiesole

The Florentine proto-Renaissance

Around the year 1060, construction work began on two sacred buildings: the Baptistry and San Miniato al Monte. Neither was based on the 'imperial' architectural style in the north known as Romanesque, but instead on very different traditions.

The centralised structure of the octagonal Baptistry is derived from Roman Antiquity, as are its dichromatic marble exterior (incrustation technique) and its formal language of semicircles and right-angles. This is also true of San Miniato al Monte, which is built on an Early Christian basilica marking the shrine of the early Christian martyr St Minias. Its small, narrow windows are not Romanesque but Byzantine (Byzantine architecture developed in Central Italy as a smooth continuation of Antiquity, and Florence did much to cherish its traditions). This also applies to the church of SS Apostoli and the cathedral in Fiesole, which were both built at roughly the same period.

The most common secular buildings in Florence during the early Middle Ages were the tall towers known as *case-torri*; indeed, one can speak of a *società delle torri*, a 'tower society'. Families developed rivalries, and the landed nobility that the city had forcibly assimilated found themselves in natural conflict. The conflict between the Guelfs, supporters of the pope, and the Ghibelline, allies of the Emperor, from around 1215 onwards resulted in constant blood feuds, and families built tall towers as safe refuges. The narrowness of the streets combined with the size of the towers – there were over 150 of them at one point, many over 70m (230ft) high – must have created a very strange cityscape. The oldest *veduta* of Florence, dating from the middle of the 14th century (in the Museo del Bigallo), gives us some idea.

After the constitutional reform of 1293, when the nobility lost their overriding influence, the towers were reduced to a maximum height of 30m (100ft) – which was still very high. Many examples of such towers survive in today's Florence.

83

San Miniato al Monte

Giotto: the personal touch

Santa Maria Novella

Painting

The orthodox link with Byzantine painting and its schematic representations was broken by the Florentine painters Cimabue (1240–1302) and Giotto (1266–1337), as well as by the Sienese painter Duccio di Buoninsegna (1255–1319). The stiffness and severity vanished for ever, and a fresh wind blew through the world of painting, with subjective depiction taking the place of objective representation. The themes remained the same, but there was a general shift from the symbolic to the personal. Works by the three painters mentioned above can be seen in the Uffizi Palace (*see page 31*), which also contains the greatest works of the Siena School, by the brothers Ambrogio and Pietro Lorenzetti (both died 1348) and by Simone Martini (1285–1344).

The Gothic era in Florence

Like Romanesque, Gothic art also reached Italy from north of the Alps; this architectural style lost much of its spiritual content, however, because of the distance involved. It was never really suited to Florence's merchants; after all, keeping business accounts has little that is transcendent about it. Gothic forms in the city's major structures were generally only there as fashionable additions and decorative motifs. But eventually the International Gothic style did make it to the city – brought by the churches of the international mendicant orders: Santa Maria Novella (Dominican, 1246–78) and Santa Croce (Franciscan, 1295–1370). The Gothic style of both these churches tends to do its soaring sideways rather than heavenwards, and the rows of square chapels are typical of the orders. After the plague epidemic of 1348, the worried populace made donations and Orsanmichele, that mixture of a church and a palace, was built. The ground floor of the church is a triumph of spiritual Gothic, while the style of the upper floors is reminiscent of the double windows of the Palazzo Vecchio. In this regard the frescoes in the Spanish Chapel in Santa Maria Novella are worth seeing: the plague resulted in a very spiritual, church-oriented artistic style.

Renaissance Florence

At the beginning of the 15th century (the Italian *Quattrocento*), a new philosophy of life seemed to flood through the city: the spiritual interlude was being replaced by a new realism. In 1401 Lorenzo Ghiberti (1378–1455) won a competition – in which Filippo Brunelleschi (1377–1446) also took part – for the design of the second door of the Baptistry. The quartet of great sculptors was completed by Donatello (1386–1466) and Nanni di Banco (1380–1421). It was Brunelleschi, however, who was to have the greatest impact on the architecture of the city. The work of the other three reflected the positive attitude to life of the Renaissance man, and even though many of the themes here were still religious, sculpture in stone, wood or metal proved itself an ideal means of conveying human emotion, spanning the centuries right back to Antiquity.

Florence's farewell to spiritual Gothic spurred on the new Realism even more – the merchants commissioning the work preferred it anyway – and in the case of Florence, this must have sharpened the city's consciousness of its antique traditions; even Brunelleschi thought that the Baptistry was actually a Roman structure. Lorenzo Ghiberti achieved international fame with his two Baptistry doors (*see page 16*). Donatello's work can be admired at several locations in Florence, including the Museo dell'Opera del Duomo, the Bargello, and the chancels of San Lorenzo and Orsanmichele. The latter also contains the famous *Quattro Coronati* (Four Crowned Saints, 1408), modelled on Roman statues by Nanni di Banco.

The introduction of perspective in painting

The painter Masaccio (1401–28) did not live very long, but his frescoes had a huge effect on the Early Renaissance. He devoted himself – probably in the company of his colleagues Brunelleschi and Donatello – to the study of perspective (see his *Fresco of the Trinity* in Santa Maria Novella) and used light and shade to create entirely new spatial effects in painting (Brancacci Chapel). This accounts for the relaxed and natural effect of Masaccio's group compositions, the perfect aesthetics of which so impressed Leonardo da Vinci, Michelangelo and Raphael. Masaccio's contemporary Paolo Uccello (1399–1475) also used the new perspective to great effect (*Battaglia di San Romano*, Uffizi, Hall 7; *equestrian memorial to Sir John Hawkwood* in the Duomo). Also part of the same generation were the great painters Domenico Veneziano (c 1400–61) and Fra Filippo Lippi (1406–69).

Equestrian memorial to Sir John Hawkwood

Emotion in stone – Donatello

Gothic formalism in the fine arts never really caught on in Florence, thus allowing the city to develop in its own individual way. The Florentine Donato de'Bardi, or Donatello, who lived from 1386 to 1466, helped sculpture break the bonds of Gothic formalism and gave it a whole new lease of Renaissance life. Apart from two brief stays in Rome (to study Antiquity) and in Padua, Donatello lived his whole life in Florence and left behind works that made him the greatest sculptor of his generation. Stone 'obeyed' him; Donatello's work runs the complete gamut of human emotion. Of his works in the Museo dell'Opera del

Donatello's Maddalena

Duomo, the prophets *Jeremiah* and *Habakuk* (the latter also known as *Zuccone*, or pumpkin, because of his bald head) display the psychological realism of his early period (until c 1430) and the individual way in which Renaissance artists rendered the human form.

The *Cantoria* of his mature period, with its frieze of running *putti*, is full of rhythm and contrasts well with the rather right-thinking *Cantoria* of Luca della Robbia. Donatello's *Maddalena*, which he did when he was almost 70, dispenses with aesthetic beauty entirely and – in wood this time – concentrates instead on incredibly direct emotional appeal.

Brunelleschi

Filippo Brunelleschi (1377–1446) trained as a goldsmith, and lost the competition for the design of the second door of the Baptistry to Lorenzo Ghiberti in 1401. He did win another competition, though: the one for the cathedral dome in 1418. Nevertheless, the suspicious members of the *Arte della Lana* (Guild of Wool Merchants) weren't too keen on the unusual project, and appointed Brunelleschi's arch-rival Ghiberti to keep an eye on his activities. Brunelleschi had already closely examined the city's architectural styles, studied the literature of Antiquity and rediscovered the principles of linear-perspective construction known to the Greeks and Romans. His architecture, which can be seen to greatest effect in San Lorenzo, the Foundling Hospital, the Pazzi Chapel and in Santo Spirito, makes use of the formal principles of the classical art of Antiquity. The *pietra serena*, that grey sandstone he used for his buildings, combines with the white walls to create the formal harmony so characteristic of architecture in Florence. Brunelleschi also used an ancient Roman construction technique to build the dome of the cathedral, placing the brickwork in herringbone patterns between a framework of stone beams and designing lateral tribunes (semicircular structures) for the building's crowning lantern.

The Florentine sculptor Luca della Robbia (1399–1482) also made a great contribution to the expressiveness of the medium. He founded a family studio primarily associated with the production of works in polychrome enamelled terracotta, the earliest of his works in this medium being the lunette of the *Resurrection* (1442–5) over the door of the northern sacristy of the Duomo. His most famous work is the charming *Cantoria* (singing gallery) now in the Museo dell'Opera del Duomo.

The Florentine palazzo

The Palazzo di Bargello (1255) and the Palazzo Vecchio (1299) marked the start of an architectural development

The dome of the Cathedral

that was later to influence all Europe. These massive, battlemented medieval fortress-buildings were originally constructed to house the *Capitano del Popolo* (Bargello) and the *priori* (Vecchio), and needed to be able to withstand attack. Built in *pietra forte* on trapezoidal groundplans, these imposing structures with their graceful divided windows and battlemented galleries symbolised the power of the city's rulers. The architects of the family palazzi in the 15th century used the same design, but in a somewhat modified form: the tower disappeared and the battlements gave way to artistically moulded ledges and cornices. A good example of this is the Palazzo Strozzi (1489), its central portal flanked by square windows and the large, rugged rustication arranged more creatively than defensively. The divided windows on the first floor, with their characteristic 'eyebrows', are rather more artistically done than those on the second. In stark contrast to the gravity of the exterior is the delicacy of the inner courtyard, which is lined by arcades giving access to all the rooms.

Palazzio Vecchio

A special role in the Early Renaissance was played by the architectural theorist Leon Battista Alberti (1404–72). Like his friend Brunelleschi, Alberti, a doctor of law, studied the artistic theories of the ancients. He wrote several dialogues on moral philosophy in which he emphasised among other things that virtue is a matter of action, not of right thinking, and that it arises not out of serene detachment, but out of striving and producing.

87

Alberti's *Ten Books on Architecture*, which was based on his long study of Vitruvius, became a bible of Renaissance architecture. He designed the Palazzo Rucellai with its rusticated masonry and its three superimposed architectural orders in the pilasters, as well as the facade of Santa Maria Novella.

The second generation

The artistic achievements of the Florentine Early Renaissance in painting and sculpture took place during the first few decades of the 15th century, and they need to be carefully distinguished from the rule of the Medici, who gradually established themselves over the course of the century. After the death of Donatello (1466), the second generation of artists already began to show an inclination towards an art of affirmation, reflected in the magnificent court of Lorenzo the Magnificent (1469–92). The courageous line-up of contemporary figures in the Sassetti Chapel in Santa Trinità by Domenico Ghirlandaio (1449–94) betrays an attitude very different from that of Masaccio's paintings in the Brancacci Chapel. The sculptor Andrea Verrocchio (1435–88) and the painters Filippo Lippi (1457–1504) and Sandro Botticelli (1444–1510) were part of this generation.

*Putto with Dolphin
by Andrea del Verrocchio*

Botticelli's Birth of Venus

Mythological figures taken from Antiquity appeared for the first time in painting (Botticelli's *Nascita di Venere* (Birth of Venus) in the Uffizi), and the Dominican monk Savonarola declared open war on secularisation – deeply impressing Botticelli, Michelangelo (1475–1564) and many others.

The 16th century

The early work by Michelangelo in the Casa Buonarotti already reveals the later master. Even though he worked for the Medici (New Sacristy of San Lorenzo 1520–34, Biblioteca Laurenziana 1524) he never lost sight of his basic principles, so well expressed by his *Schiavi* (Slaves) in the Accademia. His world-famous works include the *Doni Tondo* of the Holy Family (Uffizi), his *Pietà* in the Museo dell'Opera del Duomo, and his *David* (Accademia – copy in the Palazzo Vecchio), which was originally commissioned as the first of twelve statues of the prophets for the cathedral choir. Michelangelo helped fortify his city when Florence was besieged by Charles V's army, but all in vain. In 1530, four years after the Medici had established themselves, he left Florence for good. Among those who remained were the goldsmith Benvenuto Cellini (1500–71), whose *Perseus* can be seen adorning the Loggia dei Lanzi, the sculptor Giambologna (1529–1608), who created the *equestrian statue of Cosimo I* and also the *Rape of the Sabine* (both in the Piazza della Signoria), and also the painters Jacopo Pontormo (1494–1556) and Rosso Fiorentino (1494–1540), both considered leading exponents of Mannerism.

Rape of the Sabine

The author, architect and painter Giorgio Vasari (1511–74) decorated the Palazzo Vecchio for the Medici and was also responsible for building the Uffizi. The freedom that Florence had enjoyed until 1530 was now over, however, and the city was no longer able to provide any meaningful artistic impetus.

Pietra-dura

'Hard stone' – the Opificio delle Pietre Dure (Monday–Saturday 9am–2pm, closed Sunday) documents a mosaic art very popular under the Medici: artistic inlay work using thin, cut-to-shape precious stones collected from many different places. The Chapel of the Princes in San Lorenzo (1605) and its magnificent *commesso* panel were modelled on the Escorial in Spain (finished in 1586). Thus, even though the Medicis could not be kings, they at least imitated the pomp of the court so envied by all of Europe at that time.

Literature

Like painting, literature in Florence also experienced a sudden change during the Early Renaissance when the Tuscan dialect was elevated to a new literary level by Dante Alighieri (1265–1321). He also wrote in Latin, but his *Divina Commedia* (Divine Comedy) – a journey through hell, purgatory and paradise in 100 cantos – established Tuscan as the literary vernacular of Italy. The *Commedia* reflects all of medieval thought. As a poet (sonnets and canzoni) Dante belonged to the *dolce stil nuovo* (the sweet new style), which articulated human sentiment in popular dialect.

Dante

Dante's contemporary Giovanni Villani (1276–1348) wrote a chronicle of his native city that is an authentic historical source. The next generation opened up to Humanism, and the literature of ancient Greek and Rome played a major role in Florentine intellectual life. Giovanno Boccaccio (1313–75) wrote his *Decameron* and also commentaries on Dante's *Commedia*; Petrarch (1304–74) wrote some superb lyric poetry. Both of them collected the work of Greek authors. Cosimo the Elder (1389–1464) then played his part in promoting Humanism: at the Council of Florence, where Byzantium asked for help against the Ottomans – to no avail – he came into contact with the Greek world and in 1439 he founded a Platonic academy. His nephew Lorenzo the Magnificent (1449–92) surrounded himself with philosophers and poets, and also wrote some quite respectable poetry of his own.

Lorenzo de Medici

During his exile, Niccolò Machiavelli (1469–1527), head of the second chancery (1498–1512), wrote his epoch-making political work *Il Principe* (The Prince). As a poet he also wrote the first Italian character comedy, *Mandragola* (c 1520).

The Accademia della Crusca, founded in 1586, printed the first Italian dictionary in Florence in 1612.

Music, Theatre and Festivals

The birth of opera

In 1580 the Humanist group known as the *Camerata Florentina*, made up of nobles and patrons of the arts, met in Florence to revive Greek tragedy. This attempt to recreate the lost harmony of language and music resulted in the development of monody – in contrast to the polyphonic music of that time. Borrowing a mythological theme, *Daphne* (1594) by Iacopo Peri was the first attempt; the new style soon became popular, and in Mantua Claudio Monteverdi (1567–1643) wrote his *Orfeo*, the first surviving complete opera (first performance was staged in Mantua, 1607).

Another native of the city was the composer Giovanni Battista Lulli (1632–87) who emigrated to France and, under the name Jean-Baptiste Lully, founded the French National Opera. Luigi Cherubini (1760–1842) followed his example; he left Florence for Paris at the age of 23 and became famous as a composer of operas, oratorios and instrumental works.

Florence has a thriving cultural scene

With its great artistic, musical and literary past, Florence has a thriving cultural scene: the opera, concert and ballet events during the *Maggio Musicale* (Musical May) and the *Estate Fiesolana* (Fiesolan Summer) are on a high international level. The Teatro Comunale stages high-quality opera and ballet performances the whole year round, as well as concert and chamber music series.

The theatres in Florence usually feature performances by visiting troupes; there is the odd Florentine production too, though, eg Machiavelli's comedies.

To keep up-to-date with events, buy *Firenze Spettacolo*, the monthly listings magazine. (Although it is in Italian, the listings themselves are quite straightforward.) Alternatively, obtain *Events*, another popular listings magazine.

Concerts of popular and classical music are held regularly, often in churches or in the open air. The ORT, Orchestra della Toscana (tel: 055-242767), and the Filarmonica di Firenze "Gioacchino Rossini" are the two principal orchestras based in Florence.

The *Maggio Musicale* music festival, held from mid-May to the end of June, is a big event with top names in concert, ballet and opera performing in various venues throughout the city. Tickets are available from the Teatro Comunale, Corso Italia 16. Tel: 055-211158. Concerts, formal and informal, are held throughout the summer in cloisters, piazzas or the Boboli Gardens. The main concert hall and venue for opera and ballet is the Teatro Comunale. The opera season opens at the end of September or beginning of October. During the *Estate Fiesolina* –

Fiesole's summer festival – concerts, opera, ballet and theatre are held in the Roman amphitheatre.

Classical concerts are also held in many of the city churches. To find out what Rock, Jazz and Latin American music is on offer, check in the latest issue of *Firenze Spettacolo* listings magazine.

Theatre

To find out what plays are on, buy *La Repubblica* newspaper on Tuesday. The main theatres are the Teatro della pergola, Via della Pergola 18, tel: 247 9651 and Teatro Niccolini, Via Ricasoli, tel: 213282. Most productions are in Italian.

Popular festivals

Scoppio del Carro (on Easter Sunday): literally, the 'exploding cart'. A wheeled pagoda several metres high, covered with fireworks, gilded, panelled, tassled and topped with a crown, stops before the Duomo; from the high altar a dove, aided by a wire, swoops through the open door and strikes the cart, which bursts into flames. The festival dates back to medieval times.

Festa del Grillo (Cricket Festival, held on the weekend after Ascension). The city park, *Le Cascine*, is a hive of activity, with people chasing crickets or buying them 'ready-caught' in tiny cages. The insect has been regarded since antiquity as a fertility symbol and a good-luck charm.

Calcio storico (historic football match held on 24 June, name-day of the city's patron saint, John the Baptist, and on the Sunday before and after). The game is played to commemorate one played in 1530, when the German occupying team lost to a fierce demonstration of Florentine stubbornness, and the tradition is kept up annually in historic costume on the Piazza Santa Croce.

A colourful parade

Food and Drink

Tuscany offers some of the finest food in Italy. When Catherine de' Medici married Henry II of France in 1533 and moved her court to Paris, she took her Tuscan chefs and recipes with her, thus laying the foundation-stone for French *haute cuisine*.

Of course, like any other city, Florence will also provide you with a bland three-course *menù turistico* at an all-in price (usually around 12,000 lire), and it has its share of self-service restaurants too, with names like *Tavola Calda, Self-Service, Buffet, Rosticceria*, etc. Pizza in Florence is even sold on the street *(al taglio)* and is usually accompanied by beer. One name to look out for is *friggitoria*: these are small shops where delicious fried snacks are sold.

Tempting snacks

Allow plenty of time to become acquainted with the best of Tuscan cuisine. Even in the crowded historic centre there are restaurants (usually *trattorie*) which serve excellent food in an unfussy way. Genuine Tuscan food is a wonderful mixture of simplicity and refinement: after a powerful bread soup *(ribollita)*, a baked soufflé *(crespelle)* arrives, melting in the mouth bewitchingly with its finely-spiced filling. The menu is packed with all manner of pasta dishes; in Florence, don't miss cream of salmon sauce *(al salmone)*. Many fine pasta sauces are based on vegetables, eg *asparagi* (asparagus), *melanzane* (aubergine), zucchini, melon, etc. Tripe is particularly popular; street vendors provide various different types of sandwich *(panini al lampredotto)* often containing delicious *trippa alla Fiorentina*.

Permutations of Pasta   **93**

Insist on wine by the carafe or glass *(vino sfuso)*; some restaurants prefer to bring expensive brand-names to the table. In luxury restaurants, *nouvelle cuisine,* Italian style, is all the rage; as a rule, you won't find authentic Tuscan cuisine here – but it's all a question of taste.

Dishes

A meal usually starts with *crostini*, toasted slices of white bread topped with liver *pâté* or spicy tomato purée, followed by a choice of pasta. If you don't want to fill up on pasta, you can ask for a half-portion *(mezza porzione)* or a little to try *(assaggini)* – the Italians do this all the time, so it is perfectly acceptable.

Succulent salami

A particularly delicious snack is *carpaccio trifolato*, thinly sliced raw fillet of beef with Italian truffles. The *bistecca fiorentina* is a charcoal-grilled T-bone steak large enough to satisfy the biggest appetite; *arista* is a finely-spiced pork chop. In autumn, game and mushrooms from the surrounding hills adorn the tables, and seafood is available all year round.

Wines

Florence is surrounded by vineyards and the whole of Tuscany is one enormous wine-growing region, producing many types of wine, but Chianti in particular. Made from several different grapes, Chianti varies in taste considerably, its bouquet ranging from dry violet to fully-rounded velvet. *Chianti classico* is the geographical name for the hills to the south of Florence; *Chianti putto* comes from the Pistoia region; and *Chianti Rufina* from the wine areas to the east, on the slopes of the Appenines. After three years in oak casks, the *riserva* is bottled; top brands include *Brolio*, *Brunello* and *Nobile di Montepulciano*. White Chianti exists too: its characteristic aroma make it worth searching out. A delicious fizzy white is the *Vernaccia di San Gimignano*, from the famous town between Florence and Siena.

Restaurants

$$$

Enoteca Pinchiorri, Via Ghibellina 87, tel: 242777, among the top restaurants of Europe; **La Capannina di Sante**, Piazza Ravenna, tel: 688345, one of the best fish restaurants in town; **La Loggia**, Piazzale Michelangelo 1, tel: 234 2832, justly popular with panoramic views; **Sabatini**, Via de' Panzani 9a, tel: 282802/211559, for classic Tuscan cuisine.

$$

Al Lume di Candela, Via delle Terme 23r, tel: 055-294566, traditional, with first-class service; **Buca Mario**, Piazza Ottaviani 16r, tel: 214179, a cellar restaurant offering home-made pasta; **Cammillo**, Borgo San Jacopo 57r, tel: 212427, classic trattoria serving simple regional dishes; **Cantinetta Antinori**, Piazza Antinori 3, tel: 292234, Tuscan specialities in a 15th-century *palazzo*; **Coco Lezzone**, Via del Parioncino 26r, tel: 287178, crowded and chaotic trattoria offering good Tuscan cooking; **Le Fonticine**, Via Nazionale 79r, tel: 282106, family-run and specializing in Tuscan and Emilian dishes; **Mamma Gina**, Borgo San Jacopo 37r, tel: 2396009, hearty Tuscan dishes served in a Renaissance *palazzo*; **Osteria dei Cento Poveri**, Via Palazzuolo 31r, tel: 218846, specialises in fish.

Ice Cream

No visit to Florence would be complete without tasting an ice cream made on the premises. Always choose ice cream parlours (*gelaterie*) with a *Produzione Propria* (home-made) sign or credentials. Good *gelaterie* are **Perché No**, Via Tavolini 194, near the Cathedral and **Festival del Gelato**, Via del Corso 75r.

Florence is famous for its ice cream

Shopping

Markets in Florence are great fun. The best include **Borgo San Lorenzo** (weekdays), which offers a fine selection of textiles, leather and souvenirs; the Mercato delle Pulci (Flea Market) on the **Piazza dei Ciompi**, for antiques; and the market of **Sant'Ambrogio** (Piazza Ghiberti) for textiles, shoes, flowers and food (Monday to Saturday).

Crafts city

Crafts
To see craftsmen at work, ask the Tourist Office for their booklet *From Craftsmanship to Art* (*Tra Artigianato ed Arte*). Florentine leather-workers can be seen at the **Santa Croce leather school**, Piazza Santa Croce.

Cheaper jackets can be found at San Lorenzo

Leather
For top quality start with the designer boutiques in Via de' Tornabuoni or around the Piazza della Repubblica. For cheaper goods, try the market of San Lorenzo.

Jewellery
There is still a flourishing trade in gold (witness the Ponte Vecchio), but most pieces are now made in Arezzo.

95

Marbled paper
This is closely associated with Florence. Designs echo ancient themes or Medici crests. Visit **Giulio Giannini e Figlio**, Piazza Pitti 37r or **Il Papiro**, Via Cavour.

Fabrics
Antico Setificio, Via L. Bartolini 4. This wonderful craft shop specialises in fabrics produced along traditional lines, especially silk. Try **Casa dei Tessuti**, Via de' Pecori, 20–24, for charming silks, linens and woollens.

Paintings at Piazzale Michelangelo

Getting There

By plane

Plenty of airlines offer both scheduled and charter flights to Pisa's Galileo Galilei International Airport, but advance reservations are essential in the summer. The airport has a direct suburban railway connection with the main station of Santa Maria Novella (SMN) in Florence. Trains leave at least once every hour and the journey takes about 55 minutes.

Some airlines now fly direct to Florence Peretola airport (also known as Amerigo Vespucci airport) only 6km (4 miles) northwest of the city centre, though these flights tend to be more expensive. Italy's domestic airline, ATI, also flies here from Milan, Rome and Venice.

As yet, there are no direct flights between North America and Florence or Pisa. However, British Airways runs a useful 'Manhattan Express' service via London. American and Canadian airlines operate to Fiumicino airport outside Rome, from where there are good rail connections to Florence.

By rail

The main railway station in Florence, Santa Maria Novella, is served by fast intercity and sleeper connections from all over Europe, including the Palatino service from Paris and the Italia Express from Strasbourg.

By car

Traffic arriving from the north reaches Florence via the Autostrada del Sole (A1) from Bologna, and there is also a motorway connection to Florence from the coastal cities of Livorno and La Spezia.

Arriving by car can be confusing

Anyone with time on their hands should avoid the usually blocked *tratto appenninico*, the section along the Appenines between Bologna and Florence, and instead take the SS 325, a picturesque country road west of the motorway. It ends up in Prato, right outside Florence.

A classic model

Driving licences and vehicle registration documents are compulsory, as are warning triangles, nationality stickers, and the green insurance card in case of accidents. It's worth taking out a comprehensive insurance policy for the whole journey.

The maximum speed allowed on Italy's toll motorways is 130kmph (80mph) for cars with capacities of over 1.1 litres; smaller vehicles may not travel faster than 110kmph (68mph); and the usual limit on country roads is 90kmph (56mph). Seat belts have been compulsory in Italy since 1989. Petrol in Italy is extremely expensive.

The number to ring in case of breakdown is the same nationwide: 116. The emergency number is 113.

Getting Around

By car

In Florence it is best to park in one of the city's car parks. The boulevard ring around the city has signs all over it pointing the way to them. Since there aren't even enough spaces in the city centre for the local residents, it's best not even to try it, but instead to drive straight to the Fortezza da Basso; there's lots of parking space there. Santa Maria Novella main station is just a couple of minutes' walk away, and there's also a bus line from the Fortezza straight to the centre.

Also, for the adventurous, there's a cycle hire at the Fortezza. Bikes are a good way of exploring the historic centre, which is closed to cars and can only be driven through with a permit (though access to hotels is allowed). The police are notorious for towing cars away. Anyone who leaves their car in the street outside the centre should look out for signs saying *pulizia notturna*, which mean that the street is due to be cleaned that night, and vehicles are thus not allowed to park there after dark.

As elsewhere in Italy it's best not to tempt thieves by leaving any luggage or valuables in the car. Always lock all doors.

By bus

Most bus lines pass the main station

The bus network for Florence and environs is very comprehensive, and most lines pass the main station at some point. Tickets can be bought at the automatic machines at the stops, which have instructions in four languages; buying tickets in bulk is cheaper. Less buses run in the evenings, but there is a night service.

Taxis

These can be found all over the city. They usually come quickly when called by phone; callers are given passwords (tel: 4798 and 4390). You will find taxi ranks in Via Pellicceria, Piazza de San Marco and Piazza de Santa Maria Novella.

Hire cars

All the big international car rental companies have branches in Florence and can offer special weekend deals, unlimited mileage, etc. Information is available either from hotels or directly from the firms. It is worth remembering that it often works out cheaper to book car hire in advance of your arrival.

City sightseeing tours

These are organised by travel agencies. Several different programmes are available, some longer than others.

Facts for the Visitor

Travel documents

Visitors from the US, EU and Commonwealth countries only need a passport for a stay of up to three months. Citizens of other countries should check with the nearest Italian consulate about obtaining a visa in advance of travel. Police registration is required within three days of entering Italy;if you are staying in a hotel the management will do this on your behalf.

Customs

You're allowed to bring in as much currency as you like. Non-EU members can bring 400 cigarettes, one bottle of spirits, two of wine and 50g of perfume; EU-members have guide levels of 800 cigarettes, 10 litres of spirit and 90 litres of wine. Customs keep a close watch for drugs, which are illegal.

Foreign exchange

There is no limit on the amount of lire that can be taken in or out of the country, although for cash transactions there is restriction of 20 million lire. This also applies within Italy itself.

Information

Information can be obtained from the offices of the Italian State Tourist Office (ENIT) at the following addresses:

In the UK: Italian State Tourist Office, 1 Princes Street, London W1, tel: 071 408 1254; fax: 071 493 6695.

In the US: Italian Government Tourist Office, 630 5th Avenue, Suite 1565, NY 10111, New York, tel: 212 245 4822; fax: 212 586 9249.

In Florence: APT (Azienda di Promozione Turistica),

No shortage of information

Via Manzoni 16, tel: 247 8141. There are information offices at Via Cavour 1r, Chiasso Baroncelli 17 (to the right of the Loggia dei Lanzi), Piazza Stazione, Fortezza da Basso (1 April–10 November); on the A11 Firenze Mare and at the AGIP service stations Peretola and Chianti Est (1 April–10 November). The free pamphlet *Florence Concierge Information* (FCI), printed in Italian and English, available in hotels and travel agencies, is also a good information source.

One address: five bells to push

House numbers

Finding addresses can be confusing if the extra 'r' is overlooked; it stands for *rosso*, ie 'red', meaning that the address is a commercial enterprise. These have their own numbering system separate from the black one used for ordinary residential addresses.

Sport

Florence has no shortage of sports facilities: there are swimming pools and facilities for tennis, rowing, riding, plus an 18-hole golf course (addresses and opening hours can be found in the FCI pamphlet).

Money

The unit of currency is the *lira*, plural *lire* (L). Coins come in denominations of 50, 100, 200 and 500 lire; banknotes in 1,000, 2,000, 10,000, 20,000 50,000 and 100,000 lire.

Banks and exchange

Banks are open Monday to Friday 8.20am–1.20pm and 2.45–3.45pm. Currency exchange outlets keep longer hours. The currency exchange office at Santa Maria Novella main station (SMN) is also open on Saturdays and public holidays.

Travellers' cheques and cheques can be changed at most hotels. Eurocheques are accepted to a value of 300,000 lire, and up to 1 million lire can be withdrawn from post office savings accounts.

Bank rates vary but are usually the most favourable. *Bureaux de change* charge a commission for each transaction, however small the amount.

Bills

Restaurants and other establishments are now required by law (for tax reasons) to issue an official receipt to customers, who should not leave the premises without it.

Tipping

This is generally done even where service is included (*servizio compreso*). Hotel staff, waiters, taxi drivers, hairdressers and tour guides all expect to be tipped.

Opening times

Shops are open on weekdays from 9am–7.30pm with a lunch break from 1–3.30pm. Many shops are closed on Saturday and Monday afternoons. Museum opening hours vary considerably, and the times stated in this book are subject to change. Sights and museums are also liable to to be closed for restoration. As far as possible, we have given warnings where this may be the case. Up-to-date information can be obtained in the FCI (Florence Concierge Information).

Post

The Central Post Office *(Palazzo delle Poste)* is at Via Pelliceria 160, under the arcades near the Piazza della Repubblica (open Monday to Friday 8.15am–7pm, Saturday until noon), and there are also several sub-branches (opening hours vary). Tobacconists *(tabacchi)* also sell stamps *(francobolli)*.

Post your letters here

Telephoning

This can be done from public telephones, either with *gettoni* (phone tokens) or with 100-, 200- and 500-lire coins. Phone cards *(carta telefonica)* are increasingly popular and can be bought at tobacconists: they come in 5,000 or 10,000 lire versions. Bars and shops with a yellow dialling symbol displayed in their windows also have public phones.

Telephone booths for long distance calls are located inthe central post office on Via Pelliceria (open 24 hours) and at the railway station (open Monday to Saturday 8am–9.45pm). To get an international line, dial 00. International dialling codes: Australia 61; France 33; Germany 49; Japan 81; Netherlands 31; Spain 34; United Kingdom 44; US and Canada 1.

If you are using a US credit phone card, dial the access number of the company you require; for AT&T access, call 172-1011; for Sprint access, call 172-1877; and for MCI access, call 172-1022.

Time

Italy is six hours ahead of US Eastern Standard Time and one hour ahead of Greenwich Mean Time.

Voltage

Usually 220v, now and then 110v. Safety plugs cannot always be used.

Public Holidays

1 January (New Year); 6 January (Epiphany); Easter Monday; 25 April (Liberation Day); 1 May (Labour Day); Ascension; 24 June (John the Baptist, Florence's patron

saint); 15 August (Assumption of the Virgin); 1 November (All Saints' Day); 8 December (the Immaculate Conception); 25/26 December (Christmas).

Medical

Visitors from EU countries have the right to claim the health services available to Italians. UK visitors should obtain Form E111 from the Department of Health prior to departure.

Addresses of chemists open at night (*farmacie aperte 24 ore su 24*) are listed in the daily papers as well as in the windows of all other *farmacie*. A farmacia is identified by by a sign displaying a red cross within a white circle. Normal opening hours are Monday to Friday 9am–1pm and 4pm–7pm.

Call the Tourist Medical Service, tel: 475411, for advice. The service is available 24 hours and a doctor will visit you in your hotel if necessary. In an emergency, dial 212222. Every public hospital in Florence has a casualty department. The most central is the Ospedale Santa Maria Nuova, tel: 27581.

Theft

Keep a careful eye on your property at all times – theft is the order of the day. Documents and valuables should be kept in hotel safes, and it's advisable to take your radio with you when leaving your car.

At the scene of the crime

The main emergency numbers (police, medical assistance) all over Italy are 112 and 113; for emergency breakdown services, dial 116; for the fire brigade in Florence, dial 115.

Lost and found (Oggetti smarriti)

Tourists at the Ponte Vecchio Ufficio del Commune, Via Circondaria 19, tel: 367943.

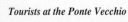

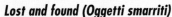

Accommodation

Hotels and guest houses

These are strewn across the whole city, and prices – even within the same category – vary considerably depending on location. There are five classes, ranging from luxury hotels with five stars to simple boarding houses *(locanda, soggiorno)* with just one.

The prices shown are for a double room:

$$$ from 200,000 lire
$$ from 135–200,000 lire
$ from 85–135,000 lire

A whole range of options

$$$

Excelsior, Piazza Ognissanti 3, tel: 264201. **Grand**, Piazza Oginssanti 1, tel: 288781. **Helvetia & Bristol**, Via dei Pescioni 2, tel: 287814. **Regency**, Piazza Massiomo d'Azeglio 3, tel: 245247. **Savoy**, Piazza della Repubblica 7, tel: 283313. **Villa Cora**, Viale Machiavelli 4, tel: 229 8451.

$$

Bernini Palace, Piazza San Firenze 29, tel: 288621. **Brunelleschi**, Piazza Santa Elisabeta 3, tel: 562068. **Croce Di Malta**, Via della Scala 7, tel: 218351. **Lungarno**, Borgo San Jacopo 14, tel: 264211. **Minerva**, Piazza Santa Maria Novella 16, tel: 284555. **Monna Lisa**, Borgo Pinti 27, tel: 247 9751.

$

Alba, Via della Scala 22, tel: 282610. **Annelana**, Via Romana 34, tel: 222402/3. **Aprile**, Via della Scala 6, tel: 216237. **Calzaivoli**, Via del Calzaiuoli 6, tel: 212456. **Cavour**, Via del Proconsolo 3, tel: 282461. **Le Due Fontane**, Piazza Santissima Annunziata 14, tel: 280086. **Ferretti**, Via delle Belle Donne 17, tel: 261328. **Hermitage**, Vicolo Marzio 1, Piazza del Pesce, tel: 287216. **Jennings Riccioli**, Corso Tintori 7, tel: 244751/2. **Loggiata Dei Serviti**, Piazza Santissima Annunziata 3, tel: 289592. **Patrizia**, Via Montebello 7, tel: 282314. **Pitti Palace**, Via Barbadori 2, tel: 282257. **Quisisana E Pontevecchio**, Lungarno Archiburieri 4, tel: 216692. **Tornabuoni Beacci**, Via dei tornabuoni 3, tel: 212645.

Campsites and Youth Hostels

The best-situated campsite is the Florentiner under the Piazza Michelangelo, with room for 500 (Viale Michelangelo 80). Others include: Panoramico, Via Peramonda (Fiesole); Villa Camerata, Viale Righi 2/4. Youth hostels include Ostello della Gioventù, Villa Camerata, Viale Righi 2; Santa Monica, Via Santa Monaca 6.

Index